IS ANYONE THERE?

Reaching Across

The Veil in Mediumship

by John Lawrence Maerz

Books by John Lawrence Maerz

TAROT

The Astrological Layout

CYCLES

The Application of Energy Within the Natural Cycle

IS ANYONE THERE?

Reaching Across the Veil in Mediumship

ENERGIZING SELF-TRUST

7 Steps for Reclaiming Your Power

OUT OF THE BOX

7 Elements for Raising a Self-Directing Child

SIGNS & PORTENTS

A Reader's Guide for Combining Psychic Tools

PLOYS FOR DOMINANCE

A Guide for Recognizing & Disarming Manipulation

NUMEROLOGY

Life's Mirror of Vibration

ASTROLOGY 4 PURPOSE, POWER & PERSPECTIVE

A Primer for the Seven Rays & the Work of Alice Bailey

IN THE WORLD BUT NOT OF IT

Heaven, Hell & the Many Faces of Enlightenment & Ascension

UNWINDING THE KARMIC WHEEL
The Journey from Survival to Compassion

CORE VALUES
*Recognizing & Surviving the Global Assault on Our Personal
Autonomy*

UNCOILING THE SERPENT
Kundalini & the Dynamics of Spiritual Maturity

SELF-WORTH
It's Origins, Faces & Remedies

With special thanks to John Edward, Jason Oliver, George Anderson, James Von Praag and Sylvia Browne whose examples, guidance and professionalism contributed so many perspectives and so much material on what to do and what not to do.

TABLE of CONTENTS

Introduction: Where Did That Come From?................9

Part One:

PHILOSOPHICAL & ETHICAL CONSIDERATIONS

What's the Payoff?................14

What Is Spirit Communication & Mediumship?................18

How Does It Differ From Channeling?................20

What Is Trance Mediumship?................22

What's Best; Trance or Listening?................22

Empathic or Channeled; Is There a Difference?................23

What are Induction and Entrainment?................25

When Would Induction Be Useful?................28

Senders & Receivers................29

Protection; What is It & Is it Really Necessary?................30

Part Two:

PRACTICE, APPROACH & TECHNIQUES

How Do You Prepare for It?................35

Taking Your Temperature................35

Clearing................37

When is Clearing Necessary?................40

Raising the Energy...43

What Tools & Exercises Will Assist?......................................45

The Nature of Spirit..50

Which Style Works for You?...57

A Useful Format...60

Validation..68

Who is the Message For?..69

Symbols..71

Part Three:

CLIENT CONSIDERATIONS

Client Expectations: The Dilemma..............................75

What Does the Client Come For?.................................77

Further Considerations...81

Part Four:

PERFORMING the READING

Individual Client vs. Gallery..86

Beginning and Ending a Session.................................87

More Tips for Private Readings & Gallery Sessions...........89

Part Five:

HEALING BETWEEN the PLANES

A Few Words about Healing..93

Clearing Environments...95

More on the Dynamics of Energy....................................100

Clearing People..101

Spirit or Entity Attachment..106

Soul or Spirit Retrieval...113

In Summary..116

APPENDIX

Appendix I: Progressive Relaxation.................................117

Appendix II: Meditation to Higher Self............................122

Appendix III: Meditation to Construct Control Room...........127

Acknowledgements..133

Recommended Reading...134

About the Author..137

When I first became aware of the fact that I could "listen to the dead" I asked myself, "Why would I want to do this?" To this day I still ask myself that same question. However, my answer keeps changing as I do. The changing seems to be dependent on my ability to integrate what I've learned. I'm pleased to have learned that I am able, yet, it was not something that I sought out. You might say that it all started by "accident."

In the late nineties I was very happily running my own metaphysical bookstore with my ex-wife, Sandy Anastasi. She was, and still is, very much involved with teaching psychic development. I have a retail background which enabled me to combine my metaphysical interests with a practical "brick and mortar" store that would support us by catering to the needs of our "spiritual" community. My approach to this spiritual world was fairly skeptical but I could see evidence of some psychic factors at work; things like knowing who's on the phone before I answered it or following my "gut" feeling taking an alternate way home and then finding there was an accident that I avoided by doing so. I took it all with a grain of salt since I had seen only minor evidence of such energies at work in my life. My own metaphysical interests consisted, mostly, of the "scientific" spectrum of study including astrology, numerology and all things of a symbolic and analytical nature. My response to people talking about speaking with the dead was, "Yeah, right, if you say so." Little did I know…

Before moving to Florida in 1989 we ran a metaphysical school in New York where a, currently, well known psychic took classes with us. In 1999, four years after opening our store, we got a call from this fellow saying he would be in the area would we like him to swing by and do a few seminars with us. We figured, sure. This would be great for him and us. He'd get exposure and we'd get a boost to our business in a venue, as of yet, untapped. He, also, scheduled himself to appear on one of our dinky local radio stations broadcasting, mostly, to our local neighborhood. We figured, based on the local demographics of a fairly religious population, that he'd bring in a few people and we'd make a little money and have some fun. Of course we scheduled ourselves in one of his seminars to get a taste of what he, and talking to the dead, was all about. We listened to him on the radio and, I must admit, I was very impressed with his accuracy and his presentation in a common sense everyday approach. As the week wore on the signups began to come in; five people, then seven, then ten, then thirteen then seventeen. Our little classroom was going to be tight. It peaked at twenty two. We opened registration to another day. That filled up too. So we opened a third. It filled also. We had to turn people away. Needless to say we were very surprised at the response in our very conservative town. We were, also, very excited.

When the day of the seminar arrived, I was excited for the opportunity but careful not to let my common sense be compromised by a wish to believe the truth of it. Having never seen him work I was sort of expecting a bit of flash and fanfare that you might expect from someone playing a part like in one of the old movies where you saw the medium shiver and shake as the spirit came through with a distinctly different "accent" so as to indicate that there was someone in charge other than the medium. Nothing could have been further from the truth. He was, and still is, a straight forward, no nonsense kind of a guy. He seemed more scientific in his approach rather than "spiritual" much like a scientist with a mind, open more than the average, to the mystical possibilities. This pleased me to no end.

He began his session with our introduction of him and his brief explanation of what he does and what we should and shouldn't expect from the evening. He encouraged us to maintain a healthy skepticism which I certainly had. He also said that he might not get to everyone but in all the sessions he stayed longer than expected and did accommodate everyone with something in each session. He moved through the room by what seemed to be random selection of attendees but he, which I later learned, was going to where the energy was the "loudest." He was very factual, accurate and extremely stubborn when he encountered information that an attendee could neither verify nor understand. In almost all of those situations the information became clear by the end of the session. I was also watching the reactions of the attendees as they were being read. Most were filled with surprise. Almost everyone was pleased with their interaction. The ones that weren't I attributed to feeling uncomfortable about being exposed in front of a group or they had what he called "psychic amnesia" which is not recognizing a person or information while the reading was in session but having it register like a ton of bricks later. It was a lot like being a deer frozen in the headlights. When he got to me I was pretty excited at the possibilities but did my best to keep my skepticism in play. He started off by asking why he was getting an image of Merlin the magician. This blew me away. He explained that my father was there, who is deceased, and that he was accompanied by a large black puppy like dog. His name was Merlin and I had recently had to put him to sleep due to pain from an inoperative ailment. At the time I was really upset about having to do that so, right off the bat, he hit a raw nerve. Holding on to my skepticism became very difficult. How could he possibly now something like that? This piece of information, something that he couldn't have known, became my "validation" of his authenticity. One of the things I've come to understand, now, over time, is that once a client "feels" the occurrence of this type of validation most of the resistance to the reader drops away and the energy flows much more easily and so does the information that comes after. As I relaxed more he went on to tell me that my father was proud of me and that he was sorry that he couldn't have been there more for me. This was true to form relative to the relationship that we had had which was very strained due to a marked absence of intimate communication. The reader also said that had my dad not passed when he did I would have found it much more difficult to go into business for myself, let alone, in one that centered on metaphysics. My dad was a very conventional kind of guy who felt you should work for a company that will provide benefits and take care of you in retirement. He, the reader, went on to explain that, essentially, my dad needed to be out of the way for me to be able to participate in the field as a career. This was also true to form since my dad never had an acceptance of, in his words, "that kind of nonsense." My session was an eye opener to say the least. Yet, I still had one burning question that had to be answered. Did he actually talk to my dad or did he pick everything right out of my head? In my mind, the only way that the actuality of him talking to my dad could be verified would be if I received some information about my dad that I didn't know and could be verified through another source like his relatives or close friends. Unless I participate in another session with him I guess I will never know. Yet, this could still happen with another reader.

This session and experience piqued my curiosity. From this point on I made it a point to explore the possibilities. In doing so I came across many types readers. Some were matter of fact. Some were theatrical. Some were emotional. Some were solicitous. Some were sharks. Some were know-it-alls. Some had false modesty and others had egos the size of a house. The people I found were, typically, no different than whom I found in any other profession. They were just people. Some had issues. Some were "clean." The important part of this is that there were no people who had any great hidden secrets that magically conveyed any special ability to do work of this style. They're just people like you and me who have a talent for something or not. Anyone can do this but it comes easier to some than others. Again, just like any other profession, it requires patience and practice. Even Einstein failed mathematics and look what he did through pursuing the skill. Enough said about ability and the "specialness" of the work. Let's get down to brass tacks.

Part One

PHILOSOPHICAL & ETHICAL CONSIDERATIONS

WHAT'S THE PAYOFF?

People come to this work with a variety of motivations. With this in mind I've come to begin most of my seminars with a question for everyone wishing to learn and develop the skill. However, I preface the question with two qualifications for the answer. I feel that with these qualifications no one can simply give a "buzzed" reason that's superfluously accepted as a valid reason within the field. My intention is to really make a student ponder their reason, carefully, with honesty rather than responding with a generic or rote response. My first qualification is that they may not respond with a, "I want to be like John Edward or Sylvia Brown or George Anderson or James Van Praag." Emulation does not do much to give clarity to a person's motivation. It obscures it with a vague sense of longing, on the part of the student, for the benefits of the medium's success. Those benefits can range anywhere between social recognition to wealth. The second qualification is they may not say that they wish to "help" people. The gist of "help" can be an attempt at personal control and power, fitting in to a popular social role of "do-gooder" with all its attending ego boosts or an earning of personal or social identity. The question I ask is, simply, "Why do you want to do spirit communication?" Essentially, I want them to verbalize what they feel their payoff would be by doing the work. I believe that every statement and action has more than one motivation. Altruism can be a very good excuse but is never the total motivation. I also believe that there is nothing wrong with having a selfish component in any of our reasoning as long as we are honest with ourselves. The altruism of metaphysics can be a mask for any number of motivations. At worst, it can be self-deceptive which clouds the potential for truthful awareness. In my classes, after the two conditions we met, reasons for learning the skill ranged from wanting to talk to loved ones, desiring personal proof of an afterlife, to just plain curious and wanting an interesting business in the field. It's also important to note that these motivations often change as we grow in our understanding and experience in the field.

Addressing our motivation for doing this kind of work brings us to another question. This one is not quite as obvious as the question of why which can be answered with observable tangible reasons. This next question penetrates our subconscious needs. Do we have something to prove and to whom? Our first instinct for an answer is usually, "I have nothing to prove to myself or anyone else." But let's reframe this question by asking, "Why do I have to be right?" How many times have we pushed an issue with someone until they acknowledged our perspective as valid? Everyone seeks validity for being a person who has an acceptable and useful point of view and therefore someone who can "make a difference." But what does that actually mean? We bandy this phrase around under the guise of being altruistic and selflessly assisting humanity. But, simply put, it means what we do or say has an effect on the world. The degree to which the effect is needed varies from person to person. Yet, can we handle being a "nobody?" Can we handle not affecting the world? "Making a difference" only becomes necessary when we feel powerless to have an effect. This is our ego saying, I need to promote a special "image" of and "identity" for myself in the eyes of others. Ego enhancement is at the core of this motivation. The person needing to "make a difference" needs to do so from a feeling of not being able to make a difference. Actually, they may or may not make a difference but the feeling that they can't is what fuels the desire to do so. Conversely, The person comfortable in their own skin feels no need to prove a point, no need to build an identity and no desire to convince the world of their worthiness. This person accepts the world on its own terms and focuses on what they want not what they feel they must change. The comfort this person feels rests in the balance between accepting themselves as being okay and the pursuit of their needs and wants, even if public opinion insinuates that they are unethical and selfish for doing so. They are okay with others pursuing theirs and offer assistance, through no sense of guilt or obligation, when the spirit moves them. There is no need to change others or the self. It is necessary to have a strong ego, or sense of self, to work successfully in this field. However, there are two types of ego in play here. The ego I speak of, here, pertains to the psychological meaning which relates to a strong, well balanced and adaptable personal psyche. This is not to be confused with the more contemporary meaning of an "ego" which relates to pride and self-promotion resulting from an inner feeling of inadequacy.

All of us have our insecurities, needs and personal issues. This is part of becoming human. The key is not in attempting to eliminate these insecurities. This will only serve to polarize, more strongly, the gap between who we think we are and who we want to be generated by who we feel we are not. The key is to accept and integrate all parts of ourselves, acceptable and unacceptable, and be okay with doing so. If others want to see us as being unworthy in some area of life, we must allow them to think and feel so. In doing this work it is not necessary to be free of personal issues but, rather, to be aware of them, work with them and do our best to keep them from having an influence on the work we do with our client.

The last concept I'd like to bring up is that of personal issue interplay. How we approach our work determines the issues our clients bring to us. For example, if we approach the work from a perspective of needing to save the world we will attract clients who are needy, helpless and incompetent or those who are proud, insulted by offered assistance and offended by the assumption that they need it. The issue behind the polarization is exemplified by the old saying "we attract who we are." More precisely put, "we attract those who mirror how we feel" consciously and unconsciously. Whether we attract our opposite or our compliment, it is a polarization of the same type of energy and the more extreme their perspective, the more extreme the polarizing. As an example, the need to save the world is the flip side of needing to be saved. Either polarity produces an imbalanced energy projection on the world; one as compensation for the other and that we bury in our unconscious. Compensation itself is a representative of our Shadow which is the image or parts of ourselves that we feel are unacceptable to ourselves or others and, as a consequence of refusing their acknowledgement, have buried them in our unconscious. After burying them, we attempt to compensate for their absence by projecting them on others. Polarizing of this type leads to internal turmoil and an inability for the reader to be able to listen compassionately to their client. To gain a greater understanding of the working dynamics of the Shadow you may find tremendous insight by reading Carl Jung's work, especially, with reference to Archetypes. His work serves as a foundation for all modern psychology.

With these dynamics in play, any overwhelming urge to do spirit communication work must be examined very carefully to be certain that our choice is not a reaction to our own opinion of ourselves. Any sense of pride or shame must be addressed and diminished through full acceptance of their presence. This, to say the least, is one of the hardest objectives we can ever attempt to accomplish and is ongoing. As we grow, our reason for doing the work evolves with us.

WHAT IS SPIRIT COMMUNICATION and MEDIUMSHIP?

Simply put, it is communicating with people who no longer have physical bodies. However, this communication may be of many different types or modalities. Some communicate by directly hearing the deceased. Others see pictures. Others feel impressions. And some work with a combination of these. Traditionally, there has been a strong sense of mystery, elusiveness and unjustified secretiveness given to spirit communication. Above all, the media has been largely to blame for how the skill has been viewed until now. It has presented the pubic with an image that is infused with a Halloween like air that borders on ridiculing those who perform the function with comic like costumes and exaggerated mannerisms and behaviors. Perhaps this was in reaction to assuage a general fear the public has of the afterlife thereby enabling them to feel they were justified in dismissing it as hocus pocus; or maybe just a poor way to sensationalize the practice. All in all, they have done a great job in creating the belief in us that its practice is out of our reach except for "crazy people" who believe in the nonsensical and the fantastic. In spite of Hollywood's attempts to maintain this image, psychics like John Edward, James van Praag and George Anderson have done us a tremendous service by showing how practical and down to earth (no pun intended) the practice can be. They've also shown us that it is something we can all do. Of course, they may feel that they do it better than others, and maybe they do but, nevertheless, with attentiveness and practice we can all build the skill to a quality of usefulness. Essentially, why should it be any different than hearing someone on the phone or watching them in a movie? The only difference is that we do it without a TV or a telephone. It just requires a different type of attention. Talking to the other side is just a matter of learning a different language. It takes listening, patience with ourselves and, most of all, practice.

First let's describe channeling. We are an awareness that sees all and knows all; but only concerning ourselves. We can call it our "Soul" or "Higher Self" if you will. It is not to be considered omnipotent as would be a creator but simply and completely aware of every circumstance connected with our own personal existence. This includes our unconscious, subconscious and conscious experiences as a whole. That is to say, the whole in terms of thirds. To that awareness within us there is no division of consciousness. It is not bound by the constrictions of time since it is much more than the mind that we work with daily which operates solely within the plane of logic. To this inner awareness there is, also, no distinction between past, present or future. All is "seen" as occurring simultaneously. In this way the integration of our lives is cognized in its totality with no divisions, segments or separations. This, also, includes the Shadow side of our nature which is comprised of our desires, fears, phobias, repressions, etc. When we put our daily concerns, personal preferences and need for a separate egoic identity aside, as in meditation, we are able to open ourselves to the wisdom of this awareness in its fullness. When we do this, it is said that we are "open to channel" or "connected to our Higher Self." Information can be perceived by us unfettered by any mental or personal egotistic restrictions. All we perceive is clear and clean within our own relative truth. (At this point it is important to mention that it is my belief that all truth is subjective due to the dynamics of perception. Absolute truth, if there is such a thing, cannot be perceived without our personal bias' making it subjective.) Many times, within this "altered" or, more simply put, more inclusive state, we sense something much larger than what we are able to explain or put into words. When we attempt to apply words, in order to convey the perception to another person, the underlying structure "evaporates" from our understanding. In these cases, perhaps, there are too many dimensions to integrate with mere words. Sometimes things can only be experienced without the possibility of explanation or conveyance. Explanation issues aside, the key quality I wish to focus on here is that the information we receive comes from only our own awareness and experience. What we receive from our "Higher Self" or through channel is completely related to us. On the contrary, spirit communication or mediumship is different in that information comes from outside of our experiences relating to others and their issues. The information we receive comes from an entity or being with a different set of circumstances, history and memories than ours. It could be from another "Higher Self" or a person "in spirit" if you will, but, the point is still that its source is outside of our experience and knowledge. We may have no understanding of the meaning or content of the message or information. Ideally and ethically, it is our responsibility to relate this information exactly as it comes to us with minor adjustments that allow us to be compassionate within its relating. In this way we may act no more than as a telephone. We will have no way of verifying the accuracy of the information since it is usually be foreign to our experience. It is up to our client to process it, apply meaning and validate its veracity. In review, channeling information comes within our experience and awareness and spirit or mediumship communicated information, comes from outside.

WHAT IS TRANCE MEDIUMSHIP?

Thus far, everything we have done has been under our own volition or "control." We have listened, felt or viewed information and operated as a mediator for our client. The key here is that we have always been aware of what was transpiring. There is another type of mediumship called trance. This is where we temporarily relinquish control over our body, through meditation or other means, that another entity might enter our body and use it to convey information from their own experience in a different "format" or style. The body is then utilized as the entity might have using its prior bodies displaying different mannerisms, accents and physiological variations. How the body is used would appear visibly different from when the trancing owner inhabited it. The owner has, essentially, stepped aside to allow another to inhabit his body. It is very similar to someone who has lent their automobile to someone else for temporary use.

WHAT'S BEST; TRANCING OR LISTENING?

That depends on what you're trying to accomplish. If the client is looking for validation that the spirit "coming through" is indeed the person requested, then the personal mannerisms portrayed will go a long way to assure the client of who is present. In this case trancing would be best. If validation is not the primary issue but the information conveyed is, then listening would do well enough for what is needed. Listening is by far the safest mode of mediumship for any reader to undertake. In trance mediumship safety is an issue that needs to be considered. Why? First, we consider physical safety. Have you noticed that if you lend your car to someone you usually get it back with the mirrors off angle, the radio on a different station, the seat adjusted to an odd place and it doesn't quite feel right? It's like Goldilocks saying, "Who's been sleeping in my bed?" If many different people borrow your car it can come back in different condition each time. This causes wear and tear above and beyond the use by one owner. Now consider you, your body's owner, lending your body for use to many different spirits and entities. Each one will use your body in a different fashion. This will cause wear and tear on your body above and beyond what it was designed for. Stress that causes aging will happen at an accelerated rate. Mediums that have used trance as their only style have been known to die young. Among those are Jane Roberts and Edgar Cayce. Second, we consider mental and emotional safety. This circumstance will occur, only, in a very small percentage of cases. Mediums that have a very fragile ego or sense of self are much more susceptible to being taken over or possessed by entities who want to return to the physical world.

EMPATHIC OR CHANNELED; IS THERE A DIFFERENCE?

There are two ideas that need to be covered here. First, what is the relationship between empathy and channeling? Second, what happens when the reading is done through empathy rather than channeling?

First, empathy and channeling occur on two different levels of density. Empathy is much denser than being in channel. As previously discussed, to be in channel, or in a meditative state, we must be free of all personal preferences, daily issues and emotions that produce an identity. These qualities, whether they are ours or our client's, create a distance or separation from the core energy we have in common with others. They are heavy and dense like clouds that pass across and obscure the clarity of the sun's light.

The meditative quality of channel allows us to bypass the clouds and perceive the energy and structure of information in its cleanest and truest form. To be in empathy with a person means to not be in channel or connected to their core energy and limits us to receiving the client's personal desires and projections on the dense, cloud oriented level. When in this plane or state we can sense the client's emotions, pain, feelings and bodily sensations. These manifestations are so gross in their nature that we are unable to hear the subtle voice of our channel or attain a connection to theirs.

The second point is that when we read the client through channel we are able to gain information directly from spirits or entities outside of the client's sphere of experience. However, when we read the client from the plane of empathy, we are only able to perceive information about the spirit from the client's perspective. We are not able to receive anything other than what the client already knows or has experienced about them. So to do spirit communication or mediumship through empathy is not actually communicating with the spirit but with the client's memory of them. This may be eminently verifiable information for the client and create a dramatic reaction since it plays on the emotional plane and is close to home by way of memory. Actual communication with the spirit however, when achieved through channel, may not be immediately verifiable and may at times even seem incorrect since it comes from the perspective of the spirit and not the client's experience of them. For many readers it is a temptation to read empathically since it produces a more dramatic reaction than what comes through channel. This can become a severe egotistical pitfall.

There is a profound difference between many readers in that they are unaware that this is occurring. To be in empathy with someone means to feel the pain or joy as they feel it. Technically, if we are in empathy with another, the denseness and intensity of their feelings and emotions overwhelms the delicate balance required for channel and thereby obscures the information we might receive through it. In this case all the information we receive is colored by the client's feeling, emotions and personal issues. But, the most important point, if we are not in channel we cannot be certain if we are reading the information from the client's memory and history of the spirit as opposed to truly hearing, seeing or sensing what comes from the actual spirit they came to hear from. Our work is to strive to learn to achieve and maintain channel to acquire the truest information we can from spirit for our client.

WHAT ARE INDUCTION AND ENTRAINMENT?

Induction is the projective or forceful polarity of empathy. It causes or induces another to empathize. That is, in empathy we are receptive to the projected force of another person's feelings, thoughts and energy. Through induction we become the projectors of feelings, thoughts and energy with the intention, if it is conscious, that others perceive them of us. It should also be noted that many times we not aware of what we are projecting or of what we are receiving. Let me present an example of how induction works.

Imagine that you are standing on a train platform waiting for a train to arrive. You are close to the edge. As a train approaches you see that it is not slowing down. You steady your footing. Why? Because you know that something that large that speeds past you that fast will have an air flow that acts like a suction drawing you to it. The suction pulls your hat, your hair, your clothing, papers and anything that has little weight and a large surface area. This force is induction. The stronger the force the more strongly it is felt. In the same way, a steward slowly pushing a baggage cart past you creates no such feeling. There is little momentum and almost no intensity. Feelings and emotions work the same way. The stronger the intensity, the more there is potential for induction.

If someone has a passing thought or feeling with no intensity, as with the steward pushing the cart, evidence of it may pass below the radar and it won't be noticed. The only way the projection can be perceived is if the person receiving the projection is extremely sensitive. However, if the feeling is charged with intensity and emotion, as was the speeding train, it can't help but be noticed by others who are, in the least bit, sensitive. So the rule of thumb for producing induction is the more intense or charged a thought or feeling is, the more easily another may empathize or perceive it, and/or, be dragged along with it. Here are a couple of examples of this. A person who has just had an automobile accident is extremely upset, or someone riding a rollercoaster is extremely excited. They are both charged. Anyone they come in contact with, especially if they are sensitive but unaware of what they're feeling, will find themselves carried along with the excitement. Additionally, someone who is in the middle of a riot may find themselves beginning to chant with the demonstrators and not even recognize what they're doing or understand why. The more sensitive and unaware they are, the more likely this is to occur.

Entrainment is where moving energies tend to line up or group together moving in a synchronized and or balanced fashion. Imagine that you are in a group of people walking to the same destination. Initially, everyone is walking with their individual pace and stride. Yet, as time passes, a curious thing happens. More and more of them fall into step with each other until almost the whole group walks at one pace and stride. To see this in a faster and more dynamic fashion, consider a school of fish or a flock of birds. It's awe inspiring to see the beauty and unity with which they move together. On a more subtle and less visible level, a group of women living together for an extended period of time will have the tendency to fall into a common timing for their feminine cycles. In nature, this is called herding.

In 1665 a Dutch scientist and friend of Rene Descartes, Christiaan Huygens discovered a law in physics showing that moving bodies tend to entrain together or become synchronous in their movement relative to each other. This law exemplifies the fact that all nature moves toward unity by neutralizing the imbalances between their differing energies.

Induction, then, is the force that coerces a unity where one moving body yields to the movement of another. Entrainment is the quality of two or more bodies compromising their movement by falling into synchronous movement.

For our purposes induction is the more important tool to be utilized.

WHEN WOULD INDUCTION BE USEFUL?

Have you ever been in a seminar where the instructor got you so excited that you felt you had to run out and do what you were told about? Have you ever been in a sporting event where the coach had the last huddle before the event and pumped you up to make you feel like you could conquer the world? When was the last time you were pumped up and psyched to do something? Some people just have a projection ability that charges and jazzes people up. Motivational speakers are masters at induction. They know what buttons to push to generate and release the emotion in you that will charge you up to be active.

In mediumship one of the best tools for learning is induction/empathy. If you are in a group in a classroom setting and someone is doing "platform work" (in front of the class practicing their mediumship skills) you are in an excellent position to feel, or empathize, what the reader is feeling that you may learn to recreate the feeling projected by the reader, from memory, at a time when you are alone and away from the support of the class. How does the class support you? When we are in a group session the combined common focus of all the participants produce an energy that multiplies where, "The whole grows greater than the sum of the parts." This energy is so strong that it almost has the effect of literally carrying you into the headspace of performing the reading with little or no effort on your part. Hence, when doing mediumship in that setting, it is, usually, easy and energizing. When we return to being alone and attempt to practice it somehow seems much more difficult. That's because the added group energy, or inducement, is absent. Then, we're left with creating the feeling from memory. We can accomplish this by putting ourselves in the same head space through visualizing and feeling ourselves as being back in the experience that created the induction.

SENDERS & RECEIVERS

Thus far we've discussed empathy and induction. All people fall into using one of these two modes. Some inhabit one state more than the other and some work equally well between the two. If you are empathizing, you are said to be receiving. If you are inducing, or projecting, you are said to be sending. There are some people who recognize when it is necessary to do more than the other and have the ability to switch. But generally, most people fall into one mode more than the other. And, usually, that one mode predominates over the other creating a few difficulties in communication. Senders may be seen as being a bit obtuse and having a hard time listening. They do poorly at gathering information. Receivers may be seen as being oversensitive and have a hard time expressing themselves. They do poorly at disseminating information.

In doing spirit communication it is necessary to do both. So, whichever you consider yourself to be the strongest in, it would be prudent to find exercises to develop the other. If you are a receiver, you might take a class in public speaking. If you are a sender, you might find a situation where you must learn to gather information from others, thereby, inducing you to learn to listen. You need the sending ability to convey information to your client and you need the receiving ability to tune into the spirits. Please be aware that I am not promoting empathy as your means for spirit communication even though receiving is an empathic characteristic, but that I am promoting the quality of listening, a characteristic of receiving, that is necessary to recognize and utilize the empathy. Reading through empathy and reading through channel both have characteristics of receiving; however, it is still best to read from channel.

PROTECTION; WHAT IS IT & IS IT REALLY NECESSARY?

In nature we see a mother duck protecting her young from aggressors and predators. Why? It is because they have not yet become strong enough to do it for themselves nor have they recognized the dangers of their new life. At some point the mother will know that the fledgling has gathered enough strength and power and that she is no longer needed to provide it. It is then that she will drop her assistance and move on. It is the same with spirit communication. There are dangers that we, as a learning student, must become aware of and develop the strength and wisdom to diminish. Notice that I said diminish. The dangers will never "go away" but there are things that we can do that will render them ineffectual on us by not attracting them to us. It is also my belief that protection is not necessary all the time since the dangers are not always present. To perform protective activities all the time when danger is not always present is a waste of time and energy and will tend to limit what it is that might benefit us were we to have the sensitivity to the circumstances. To perform them selectively and according to the characteristics of each situation when danger is sensed is prudent. Our education should be geared toward recognizing when we are at risk and what to do about it if anything.

When ducklings are young they need the protection since they are unable to and unaware of the need for defending themselves until they are trained. When they come of age, they have learned, from the mother, to project defensive tactics only when danger is sensed. Remember, the sensing was learned from experience with the mother. Since this has been learned the duckling is, now, on their own. Ask yourself, do you wear a raincoat when it's not raining? Do you keep your seatbelt on when you're not driving? Do you wear your sunglasses when it's dark outside? Silly, right? Then why would you put yourself in a "protection" when it's not raining? Not driving? Not dark outside? The raincoat will inhibit your tactile senses. The seatbelt will restrict your movement. The sunglass will inhibit your night vision. Unneeded protections will also, inhibit your sensing abilities during spirit communication. So, the first difficulty with always performing protections is that it creates an inhibition to openness that might provide receptivity to extraordinary information. (In some cases it may even grow into or be the result of paranoia.) The second difficulty with always performing protections has to do with the Law of Attraction. Let me explain.

There is an old Chinese proverb that says to acknowledge your enemy gives them power. More precisely, to offer resistance to an assault accelerates antagonism. Better to move out of the way and let it move past, thereby, diffusing the antagonism. In the same vein the Chinese also say that the best defense is to run away. But, generally, our ego will not permit this. We, usually will buy into the taunting of our pride by an antagonizer and react. This always exacerbates the situation. Hence, acknowledging our antagonist gives them the opportunity to assault us further. But suppose no one has offered antagonism? We, also, may assume out of fear that a person is a danger to us and choose to take a defensive posture even when no danger is present. In this case, much like an animal can sense fear in another animal and be inclined to attack, it is the same with us humans, however, this seems to exist below the threshold of awareness for most of us. Those who move through life in a fearful posture always attract the bully. Why is that? The bully and the coward both have an imbalance with the issue with fear. Both are at an extreme in dealing with fear. One inflicts it and the other accepts it. They both seek to neutralize or rebalance the energy even though neither will recognize the need. Since opposites attract, to posture with fear attracts the bully and to portray a bully attracts the fearful. In the same way, to always erect a protection or defense will always attract the energy you are protecting against. If you approach spirit communication with a feeling of fear you will attract that which you are fearful of.

There is another saying that says, "If someone smites you, turn the other cheek." Contrary to a current misunderstanding this does not mean offering the other cheek to be smitten again but actually withdrawing it from the table by turning and walking away. This is just another way of offering no opportunity for resistance.

Ideally, the only protection we need can be eliminated by keeping ourselves out of situations that might compromise a healthy practiced energy state. A healthy practiced energy state is one where we emanate or project health, vitality, compassion, joy and competence. For example, if a volcano is spewing lava or magma it is impossible for anyone or anything to enter or penetrate the crater and the tube. Much in the same way, if we are strongly open and in channel to our source or Higher Self, nothing can interfere with our state unless the assaulting energy is equal to or much stronger than what is being channeled through us. That level of intensity is usually not the case. Conversely, fear, doubt, shame and similar withdrawals of energy inhibit the integrity of our channel and we appear much like the dormant volcano; inactive, withdrawn, vulnerable and, essentially, susceptible to whatever "floats" by. These emotions create a vacuum which attracts their opposite or the complimentary energy. This natural attraction only seeks to rebalance the vacuum. It's not good, not bad. It has no mind. It just is. What does it neutralize it with? Whatever our object of focus is; what we're fearful of, ashamed of or doubtful of. So, our best protection is filling ourselves with whatever we feel creative about, loving of, appreciative of, etc. You get the idea. The best way to develop these characteristics is to invest in any of the arts, meditation or things that project your inner sense of creativity, confidence and well-being. Enough said about protection.

Part Two

PRACTICE & TECHNIQUES

HOW DO YOU PREPARE FOR IT?

You might say why prepare for it? It happens to me automatically in the grocery store or at parties and get togethers. It is true that spontaneous communication can occur almost anywhere but it occurs spontaneously much less of the time than when performed intentionally. Consider then, when you go to work out in the gym you don't just jump on an exercise machine and begin straining yourself to perform to your limits. You warm up first by putting yourself in the mindset for that activity and lightly exercising to get your body's functioning into performance mode. To put yourself into the mindset you first "take your temperature." This will allow you to assess what you can accomplish more clearly.

TAKING YOUR TEMPERATURE

When performing any task that is dependent on our subtle awareness it is prudent to assess our state before we begin. Feeling the difference between what we feel like by ourselves and how we feel after we make contact with another person is how we can assess what kind of energy we are working with. Why would we do this? What we are aware of through the five senses tends to be a much heavier vibration than anything we might feel on an intuitive level. The five senses have a tendency to "drown out" any of the more subtle feelings like intuition and that "small voice" inside. It's like listening for a whisper in a room full of screaming children. Eliminating the distraction of the five senses is best accomplished by dropping into a meditative state. You can accomplish this by just turning off your attention to what is stimulated by the external environment (the five senses) by focusing on your breathing; an internal movement. This, also, helps us to disconnect from the antics of the "monkey" mind or rational mind and the flow of its unending distractions designed by the "small" ego to keep our attention. Most instructors call this "turning within." However, I like Osho's perspective on this better (Bhagwan Rashneesh). You are already within. You just don't go out. Simply put, you don't attend or follow external stimulus or follow any thoughts. This is right in line with our previously described perspective on protection. The energy is better utilized when we feed our focus (the breath) rather than resist what we don't want (the senses and the mind). In this way the energy is not wasted or locked up by fragmented attentions. This creates an ease of flow and leaves plenty of energy to work with. In this state we are much more aware of how we feel, what emotions are active and how our body feels when we are "in our own space." This is the temperature we take; how we feel in our own space free from the mind and external stimulus. Now when we encounter another person, we will be much more aware of the difference we feel in our feelings and our bodily reactions. We can now better receive and assess another's energy and more clearly discriminate its quality, meaning and message.

A patron in a restaurant is served a meal. We will observe that, after they leave, the table is strewn with plates, utensils, glasses, napkins, crumbs and many more things that can be considered evidence of something having occurred at the table. There will still be remnants of the meal left on the utensils, plates, napkins and even on the tablecloth. Aside from what was left on these items we may also be able to discern what was consumed based on the scent or aroma remaining depending on how soon we sit at the table after the previous patron has left. My point is that anything we do leaves some evidence of our actions at the "scene of the crime." There is a whole science attendant to this phenomenon called forensics. Cosmic law says, "As above, so below." This means that whatever occurs on the physical level will, similarly, be reflected on the emotional, mental and energy levels. Essentially, someone who is doing psychometry on an object or environment is performing a forensic analysis. However, my intention here is not to focus on what has come before but the fact that something has come before and left a "residue." This residue may interfere with any intended action or expectation. Case in point; would you eat your meal without washing the utensils, dinnerware or linen? Of course not! You would clean them so you may have an experience free of the influence of the previous user's meal. You don't want to be tasting turkey when you're intending to enjoy a Crème Brule. In the same fashion we don't want to sit in a chair where some who was severely depressed spent a lot of time. Since physical food can be left as a residue on the dinner table, emotional residue can be left as a residue on a piece of furniture (remember…as above so below). In sitting in the chair you may not smell or taste a previous turkey, though there may be remnants, but you will certainly feel the effects of the emotional deposits. At first, your reaction to this may not be evident since we first feel the circumstances that affect our five senses overwhelming the more subtle emotional vibrations. We may, at some point, feel the effects of the residue depression as a vague feeling of depression through our day and never make the connection as to where it came from. However, if we were in more of a meditative state and more in touch with our feelings after having taken our temperature, the feeling of depression would be much more apparent to us and we could take steps to mitigate its effects. What I would like to emphasize here is that the more often we take our temperature the more aware we will be of the more subtle vibrations that exist just below the threshold of average awareness. When aware, why not change the vibration of the chair with a residue by internally generating and emanating a stronger sense of joy and well-being before we sit in it? Hence, when we sit in the chair we will deposit a vibration that will replace the depression and be healthier and more enjoyable for us and the next person who sits in the chair. In overwhelming the previous vibration with our own we are, in effect, clearing the energy of depression off the chair. When we wash the dinnerware, utensils and linen we are clearing the evidence of the previous diner. When we do spring cleaning we are clearing our environment of the previous three months of emotional and mental residue. Generally, this is healthy to do this every quarter so you're not contending with the previous three month's vibrational accumulation that might adversely affect intentions and experiences newly generated. Each three-month period coincides with the seasons and a clearing of the environment is undertaken in many spiritual and religious disciplines.

It should be noted that sometimes the vibration that has been left on an object or in an environment might be desirable to the person who next owns or occupies the premises. They might not want to clear these vibrations, especially if the previous experiences were highly enjoyable. This could account for the pleasure some people receive in wearing someone else's clothing or people who collect antiques. Additionally, clearing the environment of someone who is recently deceased may not be timely for a person grieving for the deceased and not quite ready to let go of their past with that person.

On a technical note, it should also be noted that although the energy and the effects of what came before can be cleared or erased the memory, or "imprint" of past actions, cannot. You cannot "delete" an imprint, only its effects.

Of all clearing activities clearing ourselves is the most important. Just like objects in our environment, we "pick up" or accumulate a "charge" from what and whom we come within the vicinity of. If an environment contains the residue of an argument between two individuals, our passing through it will present the possibility for us to pick up the charge produced by that argument much like walking through a field of weeds and exiting covered by their seeds. What and how much we pick up will depend on how "clear" we are upon passing through. If we are in an agitated stated we will tend to pick up more than when we're clear and detached. Additionally, in any encounter with any individual we will, also, tend to pick up a charge based on the quality and extent of our interaction with the other person. The intensity of what we pick up will depend on the extent and duration of our resonance with and exposure to the other person. The stronger and longer our resonance and exposure, the more we will tend to pick up.

The best prevention of needing to clear ourselves is to maintain a meditative state as often and as much as we are able. When we are in a meditative state there is a sense of feeling "clear" and we will have much less resonance with our daily environment or persons in it. This is what expert meditators refer to as a quality of detachment. This sense of detachment does not come from a pushing away of undesirable vibrations as this will create a resistance and, therefore, an attraction for what we don't want. Rather, this is an ability to let the undesirable vibrations pass with us investing no time or energy into them, thereby, producing no attraction and, therefore, no accumulation.

WHEN IS CLEARING NECESSARY?

To begin with it should be noted that, essentially, any interaction you have with another person will be abrasive. Yes. I said anyone. Why? Because your energy and their energy work at different frequencies and relating will require you to adjust how you deal with them. Even with your best love partner you will have to make some adjustments to relate with them smoothly. The necessities for adjustment may range anywhere from a minute "tweaking" with those you feel very compatible with to a major shift in approach with those you have little in common with. The point here is that each interaction leaves you with a residue that is "not you" after the encounter. Since the residue is not the same as your energy it needs to be dropped for you to feel "like yourself" again.

Clearing is like bathing. When are you in need of a shower? That is a uniquely individual decision. How much dirt or residue must we accumulate before we feel the need to clear? What is your comfort level and tolerance level with vibrations that are not yours? Some people can be extremely sensitive to "foreign" vibes and others can be as dense as a stone and not even notice that they've picked anything up. There are no hard and fast rules. My feeling is that you should clear as often as you think of it or as soon as you realize that what you have picked up is interfering with what you need or want to do. Let me cite a few examples and the reasoning behind them.

You've just had an argument with someone you have a strong emotional attachment to. Your pulse is racing, your face is flushed and you can think of nothing but the frustration you are left with after the argument. It's like you're spilling over and need a place to put it. This one is obvious. Retaining the residue will severely inhibit any activities which require a sense of balance. When your cup is full you can fill it with nothing else.

You've had a long day and it's time to go to bed. Work was demanding and the traffic was a bear. Taking a shower will remedy most of this but it would be best to take some action by putting your focus into something relaxing like watching a mindless TV show or reading a book or article that would address a creative interest.

Again, it's bedtime and a friend has called you and you have involved yourself in problem solving their personal issues. You get off the phone and you feel like you're "buzzing." To go to sleep without clearing would leave you chewing on their issues and being "connected" to them all night. You would wake up exhausted. Clearing is certainly necessary, but a better approach would be to not take calls from someone you suspect will be burdening you with their problems.

You're about to do a mediumship reading. You've been taking care of your daily routines and you're in a mundane headspace. Even though you're not stressed it would be best for you to clear in order to make yourself feel lighter, more subtle and aware of more than physical worldly issues. This will make it much easier to "raise the energy" as others in the field call it. Essentially, we don't raise the energy as much as we remove obstructions to its flow but we will discuss this more at length later.

These examples are just a few of the thousands of situations we encounter each day. Choice and preference are products of the mind. The moment we have a choice or a preference we polarize ourselves with someone who wants something different. This creates a natural attraction. This is nature's way of attempting to neutralize differences. Even the attraction between the sexes is just such an attempt to reunite everything in nature. Meditation and clearing are almost synonymous in the effect that they have on our awareness. The best channel we can accomplish is one of no-mind. In no-mind there is no polarity and hence no separation or potential to attract an opposite or create resistance.

So, when is clearing necessary? It's best to clear before and after every activity. This way we may remain centered and feeling like ourselves. Hence, any awareness we have will be clean and clear relative to our nature. Life then becomes the best mirror of what's inside and out.

"RAISING" THE ENERGY

What happens when we wear clothing that is tight and restrictive? Do we have the full range of motion our body can accommodate? What happens to the flow of blood when we eat foods that produce plaque in our arteries? Do we receive the full benefit of nutrients and oxygen flowing through the blood stream? Obviously, we don't. The same is true of our channel. If our channel has the capacity to be a fire hose but is occupied by petty emotions, mind debris and distress we will only conduct as much as a garden hose.

Essentially, we don't "raise the energy" but we remove any hindrance to its flow. Anything of a personal nature must be released. And anything of a personal nature refers to qualities that distinguish us as being different or similar to others through comparison or separation. Comparison and separation are functions of the mind. So, any action that releases us from them is one that will assist in allowing the channel to open wider and thereby allow us to handle a stronger, cleaner flow of energy. This can be accomplished through physical exercise, meditation, yoga, painting, swimming, running, playing music, etc. These activities, and more, are all ones that allow us to be in the moment. How many times have you gotten so absorbed in what you are doing that you lost all track of time? It's then that you are the most creative and connected to your true nature as a creator. It is, also, then that you are the most in sync with your Higher Self. Your channel is open wide. You are emanating and overflowing. You are moving with your energy.

We should also note that the people who are the most preponderant toward being in sync with the subtle energies are those who exercise their creative potential in an artistic discipline. So the next logical step for us is to invest ourselves more fully in whatever artistic propensities we have. You're not artistic you say? Well then, ask yourself in what activity do you allow yourself full abandon? If you look carefully you will find something that you can let go of the mind through your participation in it.

Right brain people (feeling) find it easiest to open the channel. These are the mystics, the artists and the creators. Left brain people (mental) find it the most difficult as they are always looking for a "reason" for whatever they do or perceive. Right brain people are more able to be in the moment. Left brain people are more likely to live in the past or future (the mind can only function within the structure of time). We need a balance of both to survive in the physical world. The next step of moving toward a more subtle perception for the feeling person is intuition. The next step for the mental is abstract. Both of these operate outside the constructs of time. Our channel functions best outside of the constructs of time. It's there that the clearest information exists.

This is also why the messages we receive through channel are not easily relayed in conventional language or logic. Language and logic are severely limited in their ability to convey multilayered expressions of awareness. Hence, symbols, pictures and music are the best mediums for that type of expression as they are multilayered.

There are many other activities that will lend themselves toward opening the channel. A few more of these are hug a tree, take a salt bath, swim in the ocean, do Chi Kung, T'ai Chi Ch'uan, pranayama (breath work) and any other activities that creates movement.

Lastly, impediments to "raising the energy" or "clogging the channel" are any activities that directly address or acknowledge what might be considered to be "negativity." These are over detailing, any type of resistance, drugs, alcohol, over emotionalism, attempts to impress the client, attempts to prove a point or any other activity that increases the difference of potential in a polarity. You might say that these "lock and block" the energy.

WHAT TOOLS & EXERCISES WILL ASSIST?

In training ourselves to do the work it helps to have images and patterns that we can use to anchor ourselves and develop our own individual type of discipline where we can feel comfortable, relaxed and safe. The following tools are more fully described and utilized in the textbook series "The Anastasi System of Psychic Development" and the CDs produced by the "Monroe Institute." One of these tools we can call a Workplace. It is an internal visual construct. You might say that it is an imagined "place" of our own design where we feel comfort, relaxedness and safety. For those of us who may not be as visual as we would prefer it may be a "space" where we hear a composite of music or tones or a combination of feelings or senses. This special "place" can be auditory, visual or kinesthetic. Each person has a primary mode, yet, we can develop a facility for all of them with a bit of practice since we possess the potential for awareness in all three in varying degrees.

Before our progressive relation, whatever form it takes, I would suggest the "construction" of a Worry Box. Into this box you will put all of your worries, concerns and issues. It may be constructed of wood, paper, material or even light. Whatever is felt or visualized, it will be sufficient to contain and retain any disturbing influences that may interfere with your relaxation and creativity. If you're hesitant to do this thinking that you might "forget" responsibilities that you feel you should answer you may program yourself to remember these issues when you complete your exercise. This box may be of any strength and size. If you feel the need you may create a lock and key for it. After all your cares are inserted, close the lid and push it around behind you out of sight. On the Monroe tapes they contain a similar tool which they call an Energy Conversion Box.

Before constructing our Workplace, it's best to do some sort of exercise that will relax the body and the mind. Any progressive relaxation will do but I would strongly recommend acquiring CDs from the Monroe Institute in Faber, Virginia. They have a marvelous program called "Discovery" leading to what they call

"Focus 10" where the body is "deeply and comfortably asleep and the mind is bright, awake and alert." It can be found online under Interstate Industries founded by Robert Monroe. For those of us that might be a bit paranoid of this type of product, they contain no subliminal messages other than what they profess up front in their descriptions. Much of the relaxation is accomplished through a process of creating tonal landscapes that they call Hemi-Sync. You can read more about it on line. Nevertheless, it is very effective toward creating a comfortable space.

After using the Worry Box and moving through a progressive relaxation it's time to construct our Workplace. This construct is to be open ended and flexible according to your needs and comfort. It can be any shape, size or space. Some people imagine a building. Some imagine a space or clearing in nature and others imagine translucent or insubstantial borders. Whatever your imagination presents you with, if it feels comfortable and useful, use it. Personally, I inhale energy and exhale a structure from my heart chakra that snaps into place around me. Later I collapse it back into my heart through a strong inhale. You may picture yourself walking or floating up to it and moving in. You may simply "materialize" yourself inside it like a transporter would on Star Trek. It may have doors, windows, be opaque or see through. The inside will be constructed of materials that you find comforting such as feathers, cotton, wood, light, etc. Be creative. Make it your own space. No one else will see it unless you invite them in. It can be plain, religious, kinky, exciting, tranquil, whatever. It's a reflection of how you feel inside. Like furniture?

Put some in. You don't? "Disappear" it. The qualities it must have are that it is safe, comfortable and completely as private as you wish. However, the most important quality is that it is flexible and can grow and change as you do. You will, occasionally, find that every time you enter something will have been added, removed, evolved, etc. You will find tools you need simply appearing as you examine the space upon entering. Other things will simply be gone when you return simply because you've either found a better way to do things or they are no longer needed. Be open to your own creativity. This is a space that your Higher Self can have full sway. In this space you can be completely open and trusting. There is no one there besides you unless you invite them. Someone there you don't want? Uninvite them. You are the gatekeeper. You have full control and authority. Within this protected space you can meditate, project, pray, raise energy, long distance view, heal yourself and others, anything you can imagine. Because this is an isolated space it will allow you full recognition of your own energy and to feel free from the distractions and interference of the "outside" world which may color your perceptions of yourself. Remember, this is a self-fabricated tool for your own growth and benefit. Use it to its fullest potential.

Another tool that can be utilized is an Energy Screen. In my visualization this is a flat screen TV that rests on the top of a table. On this screen I can long distance view people, places and events. I can perform healings. I can go back into the past, past lives, or even into the future. I can add dials and knobs to sharpen to crystal clarity, raise or lower the volume and move ahead or back in time. I can even grab the sides then the top and bottom stretching the screen to life size so I may walk through to the viewed circumstance. Doing this I can, literally, walk into any of my past lives. I can tune this screen into anything or anyone that I can conceive of in any time frame or era. The one important fact that I must remember is that everything and everyone I see will be through the lens of my own personal perception. That is, I will see them only through my own way of perceiving not as they are perceived or recognized by others. I may see things as I have not perceived them before but that vision is completely dependent on my level of consciousness and awareness at the time. Remember, also, that anyone I contact in this state, most likely, may not recognize, let alone remember, my visit. Healing can be done beneath the threshold of our client's awareness. Here we must be respectful of "psychic" etiquette and ethics. If we are confident and strong enough with whom we feel we are there will be no need or temptation to manipulate our client. I will cover more on this in healing between the planes. The Energy Screen can also be used as a door to spirits on the other side. It is a very flexible tool and with a little imagination you can think of many other uses.

Other tools consist of meditation exercises that will serve as preparation tools that allow you to proceed smoothly, stay in channel and eliminate mundane interference. These come in the form of guided meditations to, first, connect with the Higher Self and, second, to activate your Control Room. The use of the first exercise is obvious. The use of the second consists of creating another floor in our Workplace that houses media equipment regulating the volume, speed, intensity, clarity and reception of images and perceptions received in our work with the client. The dialogue for both of these exercises can be found in the appendix. I recommend that you record them on a CD or MP3 with your own voice or someone whose voice you find comforting. In lieu of that you may also purchase a MP3 of both exercises from JohnMaerz.com.

THE NATURE OF SPIRIT

One of the most difficult things to understand for beginning students is the difference between perceiving in the physical-emotional world and perceiving in the feeling-intuitive world. The physical-emotional plane is perceived through linear time. The feeling-intuitive world is not. The difference between them is dimensional. Intuition is extremely difficult to relate to others on paper or in words. To dream on various levels, which we do, comes the closest in its facility to serve as a vehicle describing the difference. There are dreams that follow a linear progression of events that we can wake and relay them in understandable accuracy, provided we remember them. These dreams occur on the physical-emotional, or lower astral, plane within the frame of time. Since they do occur on a level which would includes the mental they are easily relayed by the mind. Hence, they lend themselves well to description through language. However, there are other dreams which are much more ethereal having no reference points to any form or order perceivable by the mind. These occur on the upper astral or closer to the spirit or energy plane than the concrete, time constricted plane that the mind operates in. These dreams are extremely elusive of being described, let alone, being explained. Consider the following example.

If you can, remember a time when you woke up with an important dream. Just before you awoke, that time between the dream world and the waking world, you were aware of having "one foot on the dock and the other on the boat." While in that space you told yourself that you had to remember what you had come to understand in this dream. The moment you returned to complete waking consciousness and attempted to describe the experience in words, it fell apart. The attempt to render a description through a narrative that relied on the mind's linear sequencing of cause and effect lost its cohesiveness. You found that you couldn't tell what came before or after. The harder you tried to pin it down the more fully the understanding evaporated. The next time this kind of dream occurs see if you can back off the mind's need to crystallize or label the experience. Allow the dream to "wash over you" and pay attention whatever images surface. Let them have full expression no matter how wacky they may seem to your understanding. As in meditation, do not follow the mind. Allow it to go wherever it wants to without you following it. Just acknowledge that you are having thoughts and continue "witnessing" whatever images and feelings are presenting themselves. The mind operates like a camera. It captures and creates static images. Once the image is identified the movement stops. It's a memory of the past. The image is dead. Intuition is dynamic. It gains its meaning through unhindered, integrated fluidity. It cannot be captured in the static form of a label or picture. It comes in flashes that are fully integrated with all of its constituents. It is said that Beethoven received flashes of his completed symphonies in an instant and then spent months, even years, putting them into a perceivable form for orchestral performance.

The "language" of higher plane dreams can be thought of as being the same as the intuitive messages we receive from spirits from across the veil. They don't come to us in words, although some words may be included in the message for emphasis, but come to us as a complete experience composed of words, images, feelings, tastes and impressions in a neatly integrated gestalt. To separate out the components would deflate the meaning contained therein. To relay the message to our client could be best achieved by "painting a picture" in the form of an analogy so the client can "feel" the experience and extract its best possible meaning for themselves. A word of caution is necessary here. To become distracted by attempting to delineate the details of the impression brings the concrete mind into play and, hence, pulls us out of channel. Yet, our clients, generally, don't understand the dynamics of the process of staying in channel and will almost always request specifics. It's our responsibility to let the client know not to ask questions until the impression has been related in its fullness.

The veil between the planes is not a concrete barrier yet, for many who are unfamiliar with it, it could be perceived that way. Once we learn how to "listen" the veil begins to seem translucent rather that opaque. In doing so, we begin to recognize patterns of movement that enable us to "see" through the veil. It's much like watching a field of wheat where the wind is blowing across it. If we use our "inner" eyes we begin to see the "form" or "structure" of the wind almost as if it is a solid object sweeping across the field. Another blatant example might be if we poured a can of paint over the invisible man we would be able to see what was "not there." Even in this exaggerated and stark example, our mind, if we let it, will question the validity of what we've sensed as to whether we are fabricating the impressions or did we actually experience what we thought we did? It is the same with past life regressions. We "come back" to waking consciousness asking ourselves if what we experienced was real or did we make it up?

The nature of spirit is such that it does not exist within the framework of time. This is not to say that it is free of time. It includes time. However, and this will be the hardest part to wrap your head around, past, present and future are occurring all at the same time. That's right. All at the same time! There is no before or after. There is only the now…the present. If there is no before or after, which is necessary for language to be understood, how, then, can spirit communicate with us? That's right, through intuition and impressions that can only be understood by experiencing them in their totality. And the only way to experience them is either in the dream state or when we are in channel. However, operating in this state presents another problem to the reader when dealing with a client. Because the communication of the impressions we receive seems so difficult, our client might feel that we are being evasive in our answers due to our struggle to put our understandings into language in a cohesive and understandable form. An analogy is our best option when language is at its most difficult. Consider Jesus and his parables. The meaning was not in the words themselves that he related but in the feelings and impressions that his carefully chosen words evoked in his listeners.

One of the intriguing questions that we might ask is, "How does spirit perceive me?" To present this we must first examine how the planes of awareness are constructed. The planes range through varying levels of density; the physical world being the densest and the spirit world being the least but relative only to our individual awareness and perceptions. Everything in between is layered in degrees. To understand this, imagine, if you will, ice. It's very cold, solid and usually opaque to translucent. Its electrons may be moving but its mass is solid, inert and immovable. As the temperature increases above thirty two degrees Fahrenheit it softens and its mass begins to become fluid and clear. Essentially, it vibrates at a faster rate than ice. As we increase the temperature further, and eventually above two hundred twelve degrees Fahrenheit, the fluid moves faster still where it can no longer remain in a fluid state due to its speed, heat and expansion. It now becomes a vapor and is invisible to the physical plane. It is, now, even less dense and vibrates even faster. As the heat and vibration increase further still the vapor is no longer able to stay within its current form and "returns" to the atomic level. So, as an analogy; ice, water, vapor and atoms don't exist on planes higher than each other in as much as they exist in the same space but with more or less density. So, the more density the substance possesses, the slower the vibration and the less the density, the faster the vibration. So it is with consciousness and awareness. As our awareness becomes anchored in the physical world (ice), our vibration moves more slowly and we are, virtually, unable to perceive the "upper," or more subtle (less dense), planes. As our awareness becomes anchored in the world of feelings (water), our vibration moves faster and we perceive the feelings world and the physical world. As our awareness becomes anchored in the intuitive world (vapor), our vibration moves faster still and we perceive the intuitive world and the feeling world and the physical world. As our awareness becomes anchored in the atomic world (spirit), our vibration moves even faster still and we perceive the atomic world and the intuitive world and the feeling world and the physical world. So, you see that perceiving through the planes is much like a one-way mirror. Conquering the barrier, or veil, lies within our ability to raise, or speed up, our vibration making us more subtly aware. If a gyroscope has debris attached to its rotor the speed with which it can spin is limited. As the debris, or weight, is thrown off, it has less "drag" to contend with and gains in speed. We are exactly like that gyroscope. As we throw off our desires, dependencies and attachments to each world, we are able to "spin" our energy faster "burning off" the karmic residue and gaining clarity in the more subtle planes. One of the tools for doing this is meditation.

One additional point; the planes, in order of increasing density, or progressing "lower" into the evolutionary scheme of things, are: spiritual, intuitive, mental, emotional and physical. The mental, indicated here is the lower mental plane which, for all intents and purposes is the same density as the emotional. The higher mental plane is connected to the abstract or intuitive plane.

Back to our original question, "How does spirit perceive me?" The answer is that they perceive us much more clearly than we can perceive them. They are aware of everything we do provided they are paying attention to us. So, the next time that you think you're alone and you're tempted to kick the dog or slap the cat remember that your deceased uncle Harry and aunt Sue can see everything…if they're paying attention to you! In the minutest fashion we can now have a glimmer of the belief of how a god can see all and know all about us. Does this make you feel small, vulnerable and insignificant? It should.

Spirit perceives your client in a similar way. Imagine their frustration at not being able to get a message across to the client because they can't be perceived by them since the client is only aware of the physical, or at best, on the feeling or mental planes. Language exists on the lower planes. The departed spirits can no longer affect the physical, emotional or mental planes except through the expenditure of an exceptional amount of energy. Their plane of familiarity is the spirit plane from which they are able to reach "down" into the denser intuitive plane. A trained and proficient medium is one whose familiarity exists on the physical, feeling and mental planes. By going into channel the medium is, also, able to reach into the intuitive plane but in a different "direction." We call it "up" but it really is just becoming more aware of what is less dense. As the spirit reaches "down" into the intuitive plane at the "same time" that the medium is in channel and reaching "up" into it, the medium and spirit can then create a connection by way of a fragile bridge where information can be exchanged. Please remember that the "average" deceased person exists as such in these planes and that this is the most common way to create contact. There are, however, many exceptions where the spirits of the deceased are "trapped" at varying levels through their degree of attachment to qualities that exist on the physical, emotional and mental planes. For example, a poltergeist is the emotional component of a living person, usually from their unconscious, that is able to affect objects in the physical world. Why then would it be any different, for a deceased person "trapped" on the emotional plane, to be able to affect the physical plane in the same way? But, this is food for thought and better discussed elsewhere.

WHICH STYLE WORKS FOR YOU?

Information can be received in three different ways. We can hear it, see it or feel it. These different ways are called modes. Hearing is auditory mode, seeing is visual mode and feeling is kinesthetic mode. We all possess the ability to receive in these three modes but each of us has a dominant mode or way in which we feel most comfortable. Even with a dominant mode we may also process different information in varying modes depending on the circumstances and from whom we originally received the information. If we learned music from a person we admire and that person's mode of exchange was kinesthetic, we may have learned to deal with music from a kinesthetic mode even though our primary mode is visual. This might, also, encourage us to move toward people whom we felt were kinesthetic in nature and, perhaps, foster an assumption that they may have an affinity for music. Conversely, if we dealt with an overbearing or abusive adult when we were a child, and that adult's primary mode was auditory, we may find that we have linked the auditory mode to feelings of fear and, consequently, purposely limit our facility and sensitivity to that mode of perception as a method of defense. Hence, we would feel encouraged avoid people whom we felt were auditory in nature as they might bring up uncomfortable feelings within us. So, what this says is that we may experience many different pairings of circumstances and modes which may, at best, be mixed in their effects, but, in spite of all the potential conflict, there will still be one dominant mode that we feel the most comfortable working with.

People who are of the same mode, say visual, have an exceedingly easy time communicating their impressions with all the finer subtleties inherent within the mode. Making a connection is almost as easy as breathing. It's natural. Both see in pictures and the language used between them will be permeated with verbiage that incorporates this. Yet, when one person is visual and another is kinesthetic, their syntax lacks sufficient subtle connections to convey the fullness of meaning. Like the movie, something is Lost in Translation. This can occur, either way, with the client. This can make a session extremely aggravating, especially, if the reader doesn't realize what is happening. The client may leave the reader feeling that the reader was somehow incompetent in conveying the message received when they were, simply, exchanging information in two different languages. Therefore, it is up to the reader to deepen their experience and understanding in communication with the syntax of different modes. My experience has shown me that, through induction, this can be learned by participating in group practice readings in "platform" style where one student stands in the center of a group reading for other members of the group. If the student doing the practice reading is reading in a visual mode, and a student observing operates best in an auditory mode, that student observing merely has to "tune in" to the practicing student to get a "feel" for the visual mode. This way they can accumulate experience, through proxy, for the mode that they are, currently, less proficient in. In perceiving differently they are now better equipped to speak in the syntax of the newly experienced mode. This is very much akin to watching an artist work in a different medium, say oils versus acrylics, than we are used to working in and having the opportunity to practice with them. Now, given the new experience, we will be better able to recreate the necessary "head space" in future to work in the different modes.

The effects of perceiving in different modes are not limited to spirit communication practice. They are evident in every other activity in life between two or more people. Consider personal relationships. Have you ever met someone who you just seemed to "click" with? Besides the physical chemistry, which is the most obvious, the more subtle component of mode plays a major part in the rapport of "being on the same page" with someone. Consider employment situations. Have you ever received instructions from your boss only to find that you totally misinterpreted what it was that he was expecting from you? The examples could go on and on, however, I think you understanding what I'm attempting to convey. Broadening your proficiency in all three modes is essential to rounding out your ability as a reader not to mention creating more of an ability to be aware of life and its varied expressions.

A USEFUL FORMAT

Whenever we learn a skill there is usually a pattern or "script" that we follow as a beginning apprentice. This is akin to learning scales in the playing of a musical instrument. This sets a foundation for two circumstances. Both are focused on familiarity. First, the repetition of a pattern gives us the skill to perform without thinking of the tools we use as we use them. As an example, if we are learning to play the piano, we first tend to look at the keys to find the notes to be played. This absorbs so much time and energy, initially, that there is left only a superficial awareness of the tune being played while we're struggling with where to put our fingers. The scales give us the proficiency of the pairing of the notes on the page with the fingers that play them. As this familiarity grows we no longer need to "search out" the notes. As we develop more speed and accuracy we are more able to be aware of the tune being played and its timing. As this proficiency grows we are more able to pick up a piece of music and play it almost without a thought of the mechanics. We are, then, able to savor the piece and all of its subtleties. Second, when we are playing a piece, after developing the skill, and one note is out of phase or key with the rest of the melody, our trained ear has an immediate recognition of the difference. So, these two circumstances are, essentially, that we become familiar with our tools and that we instantly recognize when something doesn't feel or sound right relative to the pattern that we have learned.

In learning to do spirit communication we can follow a similar format. The format is a script of questions, initially, designed to develop familiarity with the skill, as explained above, and adds a third dimension; a smooth progression through the reading. This I will explain shortly. Where the relaying of the message is much the same as the melody and its subtleties, the script is a series of question focused on gaining insight for spirit identification and validation so the message will be acknowledged by the client. Let's look at the questions.

1. Is the spirit male or female? (right or left side)
2. Are they on the father's or mother's side of the family? (right or left side)
3. Which generation are they in? (# of steps back or forward)
4. How tall are they? (show with hand)
5. What is their body type?
6. What is their hair color?
7. What is their eye color?
8. What are they wearing?
9. What are they doing?
10. Are they holding anything?
11. What is their name or initial?
12. How did they pass?
13. What is their message?

Question (1) asks whether they are male or female. In the same way that we are pulled or pushed in determining which person we are going to read for in a platform style of group work we will also feel a pull or push when asking for male or female. The question arises, though, whose right or left are we recognizing; ours or our client's? The question can be addressed in two ways. You may either use the client's right or left as a directional indicator or we may "see" or feel the spirit on our right or left of the client. The client's left or right is easy to understand. Our right or left of the client means just that; our right or left of them. DO NOT feel the spirit next to you on your right or left. This type of focus lends itself too easily to getting drawn into trance mediumship. Whether it's the client's left or right or yours, whichever way you choose to use, once you have chosen, stick with it. This way there is no doubt, on the part of the spirit or guide, of which way you will recognize their response. If you start changing mid reading total confusion will ensue. Pick on way and stick with it. Once you've determined male or female inform your client.

Question (2) asks which side of the family the spirit belongs to? As above, use the same push / pull or right / left indicator. Once you've determined father's or mother's side of the family, inform your client. I have also found that no movement may indicate a guide to the client. Be careful, though, that no movement actually is no movement and that you aren't just not recognizing the movement due to distraction or being out of channel. In this question I have, also, found that occasionally a diagonal movement takes place. I've come to recognize once possibility for this as being adoption.

Question (3) asks which generation the spirit belongs to? Use same push / pull as used above except this time, instead of right or left, use forward or backward. One step back indicates the parent's generation. Two steps back indicates the grand parent's generation. One step forward indicates offspring to the client's generation and two steps forward indicates grandchildren's generation. No step indicates either the same generation as the client or you're just not listening.

Question (4) asks how tall the spirit is. Simply just use your hand to show the height in front of you. Your client will see this and get a good idea of the height relative to you. Again, this keeps the spirit at arm's distance preventing any attempt to "take over" by way of your empathy.

Question (5) asks about their body type. You may see them or feel them in front of you. Describe them as you perceive them, even if a particular emphasis is present that you don't understand. Sometimes perceived characteristics are part of the message or validation. You may even see one of your own acquaintances or relatives as a good descriptive tool for your client. At times you may have gotten an earlier indication of them belonging to the grand parent's generation; yet, they look or feel much younger. Please remember that most times the spirit appears as they see themselves. If they feel younger they will project that. If they feel much older they may also project that, however, I have seen more of the former than the latter.

Questions (6) and (7) ask about hair and eye color. You may or may not see the color. You may sense or perhaps hear the color spoken in your mind. With the hair color, remember the age factor and how that can change depending on how they see themselves. Pay special attention, however, to the eye color. As an add-on piece of information you may glimpse an expression or look that conveys and integral part of the message or quality that yields an important component yielding validation. Be aware that the spirit very often projects an image of themselves according to how they see themselves. It might be younger. It might be older. It may also be an age or presentation with which your client is unfamiliar.

Question (8) asks about what they are wearing. This will be extremely important as it may hold qualities that clinch a validation. Their clothing may hold some information relating to the message, but, generally it's a more important factor for validating their identity to your client.

Question (9) asks what they are doing. Their actions may contribute equally to validation or message. Pay attention to what you are seeing or feeling. Make certain your relay everything. You will have to pay extra attention. Sometimes we see what someone is doing and say nothing to the client believing that some action or inaction is assumed. Assume nothing. Speak about what you see or feel. Sometimes the most subtle quality has the most powerful effect.

Question (10) asks if they are holding anything. It might be nothing, a tool of their previous livelihood or a part of the message. Pay attention to what they are doing with what they are holding. They may be handing it to your client. This would, most certainly, be part of a message.

Question (11) asks for their name or initial. This can get tricky. You may see, feel or hear a name or initial directly but many times we receive a picture. It could be of your uncle Frank showing you that the spirit's name is Frank or begins with an F. You may see an animal, object, person and picture, just about anything could appear. I have also seen that where the name or initial is a representation of a company they worked for, town they lived in or worked or even a place that they frequented. I have found this to happen quite often, especially, if the spirit had a nick name that you might call a pet, a place, a food. You name it. It could be most anything. Again, you will have to pay extra attention so as not to miss anything.

Question (12) asks how they passed. You can receive the information in any number of ways. When I first started doing spirit communications I began to dread asking the question. Personally, I don't do well dealing with bodily discomfort. When I would ask how someone passed I would get pains, aches, shocks, you name it, to various parts of my body. Aside from the obvious I was distracted enough by the physical stimulus that it pulled me out of channel. So, not only did I feel the discomfort but I also lost my "stride." I had a very long talk with my guides and we finally found a way for me to receive the information. Now, instead of the physical prompts, I have learned to close my eyes and ask with my inner eyes and see which part of my body I feel directed to look at to "see" what had occurred there for the client. With no physical stimulation it allows me to stay in channel and to remain as a "witness." Some people are okay with feeling the ailments. I don't understand how they can deal with it unless they just have a lower threshold of sensitivity. Physical sensitivity, for me, was even a hurdle in learning to meditate.

Additionally, some people see the occurrence as if they're watching a movie and still others simply "hear" the method of passing. The point I'd like to emphasize is that you can work with your guides to find a way that's comfortable for you if the physical stimulation is bothersome.

Question (13) asks what message is to be conveyed. Here you have to be very attentive. Sometimes there is no message. Just the "visitation" was enough to assist the client. Messages could come in any mode or combination of modes. It can even play out in a story or a mini-play acted out before you. The important part is to relay what you perceive as exactly and accurately as you are able. Symbols should not be interpreted until they are conveyed and only after your client asks for assistance. In which case, it's also important that you remind your client that your interpretations are just that; your interpretations. In the final analysis it must be their opinion that holds sway. Also, be aware that their emotional reaction is not your responsibility to quell if they become upset. Make no attempt to refocus their interpretation in order to "ease" their minds. As long as you have no ulterior motive for how you present the message you have no culpability in, and no responsibility for, how it's received. Emotional detachment, on your part, is of the utmost importance. You are just a bridge, a "ferryman," a witness.

These questions are meant to assist in a smooth progression through the reading. The reason I suggest this is that when beginners perform their first readings there is self-doubt about what they are receiving. They get "lost" in the question and seem like they've disappeared inside themselves. As this occurs they begin to question the information that they receive and in participating in the details, they slowly slip out of channel. The tendency is to ask the question again and again and ponder whether they received the proper answer or even if the received a response from spirit. They question whether what they received was just their imagination or did they really receive what they thought. In platform sessions I urge the readers to ask the question, accept the first impression they receive, even if, and especially, if it makes no sense to them, and proceed on to the next question. My intention is to eliminate any tendency toward thinking between question and response. If they move fast enough through the questions they are, generally, unable to think on or dwell on the answer and are, therefore, prevented from being pulled out of channel by their minds. Once they have trained themselves to pass information, as it is given, and follow the questioning process, they develop a familiar feeling with its progression. As this occurs they begin to feel no longer that they are lost and uncertain about the responses they receive. Essentially, they have trained themselves to trust in their own flavor of intuition and not be sidetracked by mental doubt. Remember, the mind wants to maintain itself as the dominant process. Information is received from spirit through intuition. The mind has to be trained when to input its influence and when to "back off" in favor of another mode of awareness. This system of questions is an attempt to accomplish just that; to forge a place for intuition to be received and operate as a useful tool.

The first people to look for validation are, usually, scientists and people from Missouri (the show me state). Validation is, without a doubt, important, but why? Do you believe everything everyone tells you? Why not? The question that most of us ask ourselves is, "Why should we believe them? What is it that they have done, said or portrayed that would earn our trust of what they say?" The more experience we have with people the more we understand that not everyone tells the truth. Why they don't is not as important as understanding that this is so. In this materialistic world we have come to expect some kind of verification of truthfulness in every aspect of life. Having been exposed to advertising we want to see something work. Having been exposed to politicians we want to see their promises materialize. Having chosen to associate with people that we have found to be truthful we are more likely to believe what they tell us. This group may or may not include family. Within each of us there is a threshold or standard that must be met before we will have complete faith in someone or something. In spirit communication this standard is met by hearing something about ourselves and/or the spirit that no one else could possibly know. When this bar is reached it's like the dam opening and all the following information is, usually, accepted at face value. The client is, now, open to receiving what they have come for. If this bar is not reached by the reader, the client will spend more time trying to assert the authenticity of the reader than listening to the information coming through from the spirit. Their hesitancy will act as a block by taking their attention and energy. Even if the information is valid it may never impress the client due to their mistrust and tendency to wait for that specific piece of information that will unlock their belief. Hence, it is imperative that the reader strive for that piece of validity by relaying everything received, no matter whether it's understood by them or not and no matter how trivial the piece of information seems. This trust can be unlocked through the utterance of one word or exposure of the smallest detail. We can't predict where the opening will be. We must trust our Higher Self to provide the right information to accomplish this. Sometimes, not accomplishing validation is what is necessary to dissuade clients from developing a dependency on direction provided by outside spirits as an encouragement to rely on their own inner voice. We must all make our own decisions and be responsible for the consequences. We must all strive to provide a door for validation either way.

WHO IS THE MESSAGE FOR?

Sometimes one of the hardest things for a client to accept is that the message is not meant for them. We all assume that whatever message comes through is specifically meant for us. This is a natural assumption since we are part of a culture that grew up in the "me" generation. But, what if we can't make sense of the message we get? What if the indicators tell us that it better fits someone we know? We can accept it as being for a relative since they are part of our "clan" but what if it sounds like the details fit Joe who works at the corner grocery market? To us he's just an acquaintance. What then? It seems unlikely but it happens more times than you might think.

Imagine yourself on an expressway with a specific destination. The place you would like to get to is actually between exits. To get there you must take any exit that is close to your destination and find your way through the backstreets. Spirit communication operates the same way. Suppose the message you, as a spirit, want to get across cannot be delivered directly to the person you want because there is no "exit" available that goes directly to that person. What to do? In terms of energy, your intended recipient may not be open enough to hear the message, may never have considered going to a spirit communicator or, they may not even have a belief in such things. To find a way around this you might find a neighbor, relative or acquaintance that is open. This would be the nearest person to your intended contact that does have an "exit" or connection to that person. Hence, the path of least resistance that consumes the least amount of energy that arrives at your intended recipient. You must be flexible and act just like a mountain stream flowing down the side of the mountain following the path of least resistance. If the client recognizes that the message is for someone other than them or their family and, yet, agrees to convey the message, then, your mission is accomplished. If the client who receives the message is not able or willing to deliver it, the flow stops. The message is stuck like the mountain stream pooling up before it has a chance to get to the bottom. It, then, must stay with them until an opening occurs or the spirit must find another avenue.

As a reader, it is a challenge to convince others to convey a message to another who may have objections to doing so for a variety of reasons. The most obvious reason is that they might feel foolish in doing so. The best you can do is to address their compassion as to how they, as the recipient, might feel in receiving such a message. It might be just the thing needed to ease their suffering. You have no control or responsibility as to whether it is delivered or not. All you can do is pass it on. Do your best, then move on.

SYMBOLS

Relative to symbols, symbolism and whether to or how to interpret them has been discussed as to the dangers of getting too involved. I have discussed the cautions involving interpretation emphatically since the usual tendency is for the reader to easily become bogged down by the details and lose their channel in doing so. Yet, there is still a need to interpret them which must include some measure of skill and accuracy that can be developed.

Why do we use symbols? First, our communication here, on this plane, is primarily verbal or written. It is extremely limiting in attempting to impart the depth of meaning that can be perceived, collectively, through many levels. Second, the spirits, generally, don't use "verbal" unless the reader is primarily an auditory receiver. Our tendency is to "listen" in one mode; auditory, visual, tactile, olfactory or feeling. Once we receive in one mode, the first one we sense information through, we have the tendency to shut down or ignore the others. This being said, it is important to not "lock down" on one type of "listening" once we believe we have received pertinent information. The next piece might be most easily, and applicably, conveyed in a different mode.

We have explored the fact that symbols can be received through a gestalt of combined modes using pictures, smell, sounds, music, feelings and more. It is necessary to be aware that even in one mode these symbols can be perceived differently. Consequently, as the message proceeds we can even miss symbols if we are not open to changing our perspective of them even in mid-stream. In some cases it might feel like we are being subjected to the misdirection of slight of hand. Let's take a look at these variations in order to be aware of what to look for. I am aware of five dominant "formats."

OBJECT TO OBJECT: Sometimes "a duck is just a duck." In this form the meaning of the object represented is actually the object shown. This is direct and the most obvious where we would not look for a deeper meaning. We might even feel that this is too easy and read into the image much more than is actually represented.

OBJECT TO ACTION: In a prior reading I felt that I was torn between two spirits "speaking" at the same time. I became very frustrated at attempting to distinguish which characteristics belonged to which. The clarity of the reading was becoming muddled as I became more confused and I felt I was losing the channel. At that point I blurted out loud, "Which spirit am I communicating with?" At that instant I received an image of a tool used by road laborers who chop away at hard ground and blacktop. It was shaped like a double sided ax only with long pointed tips. When I described the image to the group I was told that it is called a "pik." After pondering the image for a moment I realized that the spirits were telling me to "pick" one and move on from there. They weren't giving me an image to interpret; they were giving me an action to perform. Imagine my surprise. It taught me about being open to perceiving things in a different light and with a more open mind.

OBJECT TO TIME: Occasionally, I will receive an image of a mirror. This usually occurs when I've asked my client about a circumstance relating to time. I've come to understand, or at least relate the symbol, as a need to "look back" in time as we would reflect on our history and experiences. More often than not it would refer to time. The other times it would refer to a physical mirror or as a suggestion for the client to look at themselves for the answers they seek. I have also received a book with turning pages. Depending on which way the pages were turning would tell me which direction to look; toward the past or the future. The more pages that were turned, the further back or forward we were to look.

OBJECT TO ANALOGY: When a client asks for clarification on how a situation occurred or how it was perceived by the spirit, I sometimes had a flash of a whole story or scenario portraying a relative, friend or enemy in my past that would show me detail paralleling the spirit's situation in order to clarify their perspective. The fact that I experienced the situation myself gave me what I needed to explain it fully to the client. Sometimes it would be too abstract for the client to understand and sometimes I lacked the ability to present it clearly. Occasionally, the story I received came from the client's past and, in that case, it became very confusing discriminating whether we're receiving an analogous story or a new message in itself. This type of "format", in my opinion, is the most "slippery" and requires us to really stay on our toes.

OBJECT TO CHARADES: This "format" to me is the most fun. It takes the sound of a word and connects it to a spelling that has a completely different meaning. Some of you may feel this is stretching a point. You might get a vision of "Luke" Skywalker insinuating that you must "look" or you may receive a picture of "ranch dressing" encouraging you to conjure the image of a "cowboy's attire." If you can approach the images with a playful attitude it can be a lot of fun, especially, in the "aha!" moments!

I'm sure there are many more ways to look at how we receive information. Some of the spirits and guides can get pretty creative. If you miss a few, don't get frustrated. Just chalk it up toward experience and remember the style or "format" for another time. It's all about developing new and innovative ways of being aware. If you're not too invested in the results, and by now you shouldn't be, you can have a lot of fun playing with new presentations. Laughter is an opening energy and serves to strengthen the channel.

Part Three

CLIENT CONSIDERATIONS

CLIENT EXPECTATIONS: THE DILEMMA

Throughout exposure to different readers, books, lectures, TV shows and the like our clients have developed a wide variety of expectations for how a session is to progress. Depending on what a person feels is important for their session, the emphasis can differ radically. For those who are scientifically minded the accuracy of details will be extremely important. For those who are emotional in nature, the "feel" of the reading will be most important. For those who are status conscious, the presentation and the reader's reputation will be most important. For others it might be most important that they "like" the reader. Attempting to accommodate all these variations and more could become overwhelming, especially, for the unseasoned reader. It is important that we are aware of all these variations in as much as we can glean how the client will perceive what we present. Still, in light of these considerations, the most important struggle for the reader will be to determine the balance between detail and depth of information presented in the session. Let me explain why there's a difference.

Generally, we westerners have become conditioned to live with a materialistic "show me" world approach to events and circumstances yielding a detailed and pragmatic perspective. So, we come to expect others to relate to us in a similar way that allows us to gain information that can be applied to specific needs. Life also utilizes a tremendous amount of concentrated energy in order to exist in a physical form that dissipates when we discorporate (die). Conversely, spirit, who is no longer locked into the polarity oriented and time constricted world of the mind, has gone through, or is going through, a metamorphosis that allows them to function in a world that is more nebulous and inclusive in its perspective of life. Communication and "messages" occur in a format which is much more of a Gestalt of information rather than individually specific facts. Hence, to economize energy and get the most information across to us the "living" with the least expenditure, they will tend to layer the communication with as many levels and perspectives as possible in one projection. Remember, they no longer have the concentrated energy that they had when they had a physical body. They are working with a much softer and more subtle supply of energy than we are. Communicating in this way has the tendency of softening or blurring the focus of the information thereby deflating the impact, and sometimes the verifiability, of what is presented. Hence, the dynamism of focus is sacrificed and the information is presented in a less focused, multifaceted, depth oriented and all-inclusive projection, much like a wave. The result of the message is like waking up from a dream with an understanding that depends on the integration of multileveled dimensions and attempting to render it to another with only the words available in a language that's one dimensional. This can be very frustrating to express since the message, or dream, is much more inclusive than words can relate with any fullness. Yet, here sits the client looking for specific facts that address one dimensioned personal issues. How do we bridge the gap between what we're receiving and what the client might wish for or expect?

I cannot offer any one pattern that will satisfy the needs of each reader, especially, since the way each one receives is going to vary in style, mode, approach and experience. I can say that as you get more comfortable with your own style that you will develop a balance point between the two dimensions (specific facts and inclusive nebulousness). Additionally, this will continuously morph as you grow in ability.

WHAT DOES THE CLIENT COME FOR?

There are many reasons that we have for doing things. They vary from person to person, family to family and culture to culture. They may be traditional or completely unconventional. Most of the reasons that we are aware of, however, are conscious, surface issues that are connected to the details of living our lives daily. Beneath the surface practicalities we are all the same; motivated by our need for love, attention, recognition, assurance and a feeling of having a place to belong. In short, we need to feel we have a place in the world where we are needed. When our world is changed by the departing of someone we feel is an integral part of that world our cues for living go through a shift. We feel, in a sense, lost and in need of new "anchoring." We can feel a whole host of emotions as a result of feeling like we were "left hanging;" because we were unable to establish a "plan" for the future without the deceased. Following is a list of feelings that can motivate a client to come to us for our help to resolve.

CLOSURE: If a client feels that something was left undone with someone who has passed on, we can consider them missing closure. That can be something as simple as not having been able to say goodbye to something more complex involving their wishes for the disposition of assets, possessions, "dying wishes" or even giving their permission for the client to move on without them.

FORGIVENESS: If there were circumstances that created ill feelings between the client and the deceased producing guilt or regret, the client and the deceased may need to receive or give forgiveness (sometimes the spirit seeks it from the client). These kinds of feelings can fester just under the threshold of consciousness affecting every emotional interaction the client has and even to go as far as to be self-punishing to the point of depriving oneself of future healthy relations through a feeling of being undeserving. Fear generated thinking, regret and guilt are extremely powerful compelants toward unhealthy and irrational actions and, unresolved or unacknowledged, can live beneath the threshold of consciousness for years and even lifetimes.

ARE THEY ALRIGHT? Sometimes a client just needs confirmation to know that the departed are safe and in a good place. It might come from a love for the departed or even a twinge of guilt as to how they handled themselves before they left.

CONTINUE the CONNECTION: In my travels I came across a lady who was unable to acknowledge the loss of her son. She became a psychaholic or a spirit communication "junkie." Whenever I had a reader's fair at my bookstore she came repeatedly and saw as many spirit communicators as she could afford attempting to make contact with her son. This was an indication of problems that go much deeper that what we, as readers, should be required or are equipped to handle. We can only make recommendations to seek professional help and limit her visitations to our resident readers.

ENERGY: Being in channel can be exhilarating for the reader and the client. A strong channel emanates a field of energy around the reader and clients who enter this field and they, literally, feel a "rush" just by inhabiting the space. The effect may show itself through a client who does everything in their power to prevent the reading from terminating. They may constantly ask questions requiring the reader to be in channel to acquire the information that they ask for. They may even go as far as taking out their checkbook at the end of the reading and perpetuating the session through idle conversation while stalling the writing of the check. Most of the time, the stalling occurs below the client's threshold of awareness. They don't know why they can't leave. All they know is that they feel good and don't want the session to end. As a reader, the best thing that you can do is to terminate the channel. This can easily be accomplished by donning a hat closing the crown center. There are many other actions the reader can take to "switch off" the supply and terminate the session; however, I don't want to go into them here.

CURIOSITY: Much like walking into a store that seems to have a novel selection of stock, a client may simply come to sample and experience what you have to offer. If you've never had a reading before it can be intriguing. You may feel a little like a bug under a microscope but that's just part of a scientific and inquisitive mind. If you're seasoned with channeling you probably will never notice.

PERSONAL VALIDATION: In some cases the purpose of validation is not to verify that who is being communicated with is actually the spirit named. The validation may just be for the client to actually verify to themselves that the process is real. Many people have never heard of spirit communication much less have a belief in it. We all have beliefs and all those beliefs have come from personal experience or hearsay from those we trust. It's only natural that we should seek some evidence confirming what we see and hear as being valid. There are many times that circumstances fall so far outside our sphere of our experience that we don't trust our own eyes and ears because it's so different from what we're used to. Hence, we seek someone whose domain it is; you, the reader.

There may be variations and combinations of these reasons but these are, generally, the ones that are the most common. Whatever the reasons may be, being aware of them can be very helpful in understanding what the client may need in terms of responses or direction. However, it's important not to get caught up in them simply so your client might feel like they've gotten a "good reading." Your objective, first and foremost, is to relay what you get as faithfully as you possibly can without any personal embellishment. In the long run you will feel "cleaner" about the reading you've done.

In doing readings, especially as a beginner, we have urges to say things to our client that, at the time, might not seem relevant to what's being covered. We will remember that we must be open to pass on information, for the sake of our client, who may have an understanding of relevance about the information that we don't. There is a thin line between passing on information that we have no understanding of and giving information that might be coming from our unconscious need to make a "difference." If we can be honest with ourselves in that we have absolutely no understanding of what has "come through" then it's probably safe to say that it's something the client might have an understanding of. There are other times, however, that we have our doubts as to where the information is coming from, us or the spirit, that we must make a judgment as whether to make comments about the information or not. In order to determine that we are not rationalizing an ego generated comment there are a few questions that we can ask ourselves as the doubtful information presents itself:

First, are your comments being presented coming from a feeling of kindness and compassion? Comments that produce shocks or jolts are, generally, not tendered by spirit. They are a human foible intended to elicit an emotional response from the client creating distress and releasing energy. If your comment "drops a bomb," chances are it comes from your own personal need for recognition and attention (energy).

Second, is the comment you are about to make true? If it is and it is not something that you would feel as if you were patronizing the client's current self-image or that of the communicating spirit, phrase it in a way that it can be viewed as a means to improve their situation or perspective. There is always a constructive way to present alternative strategies.

Third, is the comment something that is useful? Is it something that the client can use to improve their present feeling about their situation? Generally, there is a reason for everything that we say. Be sure that what you say is something that will apply, constructively, to your client's Self-Trust and confidence in their ability to handle their current circumstances. Everyone thrives on encouragement. No one wants criticism without alternatives. Be truthful, kind and compassionate and you and your client will both benefit.

As you may have gleaned thus far there is a tremendous amount of understanding required to handle your client in a professional and compassionate manner. We may already have some understanding and some we must gain through experiencing and dealing with our clients over a period of time. Some of us may be better at dealing with specific types of situations over others but there is always something for all of us to learn. Your style and the issues that you are the most familiar with will determine what kind of issues and clients will be attracted to you. Remember, we teach what we most need to learn. We attract whatever we have the most resistance to and whatever is just below the threshold of our awareness. It's like a catsup bottle. Whatever was last to go in is the first to come out. Like an onion, the taste, texture and structure of each layer is dependent, sequentially, on what came before.

If you've had counseling training in the past; it's all the better. If not, it would behoove you to acquire some books that teach the skill; not so much the ones that give a scientific approach but those with a more humanistic perspective. Additionally, any books that deal with grief and loss would be a good choice just so you will be able to develop a comprehension of the kind of headspace many clients might come to you in. A traditional book on the subject, old but still very much on the mark, is "On Death and Dying" by Elizabeth Kubler Ross. It gives a very clear description of the stages everyone goes through after a loss. Every loss is an opportunity to break patterns and develop new skills for dealing with current issues. Look at the books that have given you the most insight in dealing with your own internal issues and losses and, odds are, they will be of equal value to your clients, especially, in light of the fact that we attract who we are and what we are dealing with. There should be very little concern with feeling ill equipped to handle the clients drawn to you. After all, like attracts like. What I would like to caution you on is that you should be careful not to be too cocky in thinking you've got it all in the bag. In the event that you draw people to you who need more than you are able to provide at the moment, be certain you have a list of names and numbers of professionals that you can recommend clients to that are beyond your means to handle, and don't be too proud to say so. You are not God. Your clients have come to you for information NOT to be cured or fixed AND it is not your responsibility to do so. Additionally, have a list of telephone "hotlines" available for those needing immediate attention for crisis situations. Lastly, always expect the unexpected.

Occasionally, a client will come to you for more than one session. You must use your own judgment to determine whether they are working out an issue through your ability to connect with their lost relations or they are just unable to let go. Once their return becomes more than two or three sessions you should look deeper for indications of dependency issues stemming from fear of their progressing beyond the current situation. Have your list of professionals readily on hand. In this case they will probably need a grief counselor. It's imperative that you learn and accept the limits of your counseling skills.

In any counseling capacity it's inevitable that, at some point, we will be dealing with a client's fear, anxiety, anger and depression. I have no rote pattern for handling any of these other than to remain aware and be as compassionate as you are able so as to make things easier for your client to feel comfortable. Put yourself in their place. How would you feel given the circumstances they are presenting you with? Remember, not everyone will react the same way given what we do. Allow for variations in culture, familial background and upbringing. Judgment and labeling will be your worst enemy. Remain detached and accepting. Pay close attention to what your client brings you. On some level you yourself are dealing with or have dealt with a variation on their theme. Otherwise, they wouldn't have been attracted to you instead of a different reader. Assess your own similarities after the reading. This will allow you to work with impartiality and remain in channel.

Part Four

PERFORMING the READING

INDIVIDUAL CLIENT VS. GALLERY

Depending on which setting you perform the reading in; there will be different approaches to use. If you are working with a client in a private environment, there are no restrictions for you to be aware of other than what has been discussed thus far relating to your professional etiquette and behavior in regard to your client's comfort and dignity. Whatever they say you know you must hold in the strictest of confidence. However, in a gallery style reading (reading a client in a group setting) you must be much more discreet with how you phrase information you are divulging. A client's personal privacy needs are going to vary from client to client. You must be careful to avoid conversations and information that may, in any way, embarrass or make your client feel threatened. Some clients are very open with their lives in front of others. Some are much more protective of their private lives. When considering privacy always err on the side of discretion. If you are doubtful as to whether they would feel publicly threatened or embarrassed by what you might reveal you must hold the information for a later time, in private, yet, communicate to them that this information awaits them when the group is out of earshot. For information that you feel might be more private you can hold and suggest that the client meet with you after a gallery session.

Beginning and ending a session seems to be the most difficult for a new reader until they develop their "routine." A private session is fairly easy. Upon meeting, introduce yourself if they don't already know you. Then, small talk is simple when you're dealing one on one; weather, traffic, directions, etc. All these things can "break the ice" for opening a communication line. Once you've established a connection, thank them for coming and tell them how you will proceed. That includes telling them about being quiet for a few moments while you go into channel. Don't feel pressured or in a hurry. If you do you're feeling, either, their anxiety and anticipation or your own. Just move through both. You've just established how you are going to handle the session and who's in the lead has already been established. Generally, clients feel comfortable when the reader takes charge and lays out a "plan." Ask if there are any questions and then begin. Simple enough, right?

Ending a private session may be a little trickier. Assuming you have done a good reading, and I'm assuming that you have, you must thank the client for the opportunity of working with them and tell them that the session has ended. You can do this by telling them that the spirits have moved on, their time is up or that your next client will be arriving soon and that you must prepare. (Remember, you're still in charge.) Most clients will acknowledge this and move on. Some clients may be reluctant to leave as they have gotten a taste of what it feels like to be in channel. It is important that you close your channel and allow them to become "reabsorbed" with the physical world. As discussed before, your client might not even know why they don't want to leave, but, in any case, keep the lead and encourage them to do so in the most polite and compassionate manner that you are able. In time you will become skillful in doing this smoothly.

Beginning and ending a group session is a little different. New readers may find beginning a little more intimidating since they don't always have a clear or focused acknowledgement from the group while performing their introduction. It would be wise to develop a pattern or routine for moving through the introduction and your plan for the group so you don't have time to feel self-conscious. I have found that, for me, the easiest way to get over the feeling of uncertainty while beginning is to preset a monologue. First I introduce myself, tell them where I'm from and how I am going to proceed with the session. I ask if there are any questions, answer them and then begin. So, I've moved in, established the lead and will keep it as long as I stay focused on what I am there to do. I've also told them about the quiet time I will take while I go into channel. Most people will feel comfortable as long as they have an idea of what's coming next. I have also found that it is helpful to utilize the group's excitement and anxiety to power my channel. Once a group session is "on the roll" it feeds the channel and makes it easier to keep it open as compared to when I am in a private session. However, this is not any reason for me to drop diligence in maintaining the channel. Stay focused and keep moving.

Closing a group session is a little different. Depending on the energy level, three things must happen. First, you must decide when it's time to end, second, you must allow any last minute questions (you might have to set a limit) and third, tell the group that the session is officially concluded but they may remain and converse about what they received as long as time and space allow. You will surely receive questions and confirmations directed at you privately. On some occasions you may, also, have to use poise and tact to prevent from being maneuvered back into channel to continue the readings.

MORE TIPS FOR PRIVATE READINGS & GALLERY SESSIONS

Up to this point I have covered the more major concerns of doing spirit communication whether in private or gallery. In either setting there are a whole host of details that should be addressed as we become more familiar with conducting and running our own sessions. I consider them much like refinements that an artisan begins to become aware of and address after they have developed rudimentary skills in utilizing their tools. Like a sculptor, our creation is now standing and has the main body of work in place awaiting the detailing that give it it's character and style. They vary in importance but, none-the-less, are required for the clean transmission of information. Let's move on.

Posture is important for a couple of reasons. It should be attended whether sitting or standing. As an example, let's picture a garden hose. If it's kinked, the water will have a difficult time passing through it if at all. The kundalini channel in our body, called the Sushumna, is a lot like that hose in that if it is bent the life force and kundalini will have a difficult time ascending through it. In meditation, which is akin to channeling, we are encouraged to have straight posture so as to allow these energies to ascend and descend through the body easily. Whether the physical attributes of good posture affects us as much as our attitude remains to be seen, yet one of the earmarks of doubt, fear and poor self-confidence is poor posture. People, who have or project a feeling of self-confidence, invariably exhibit good posture. We recognize this and respond accordingly whether we are conscious of it or not. We usually find ourselves applying respect and admiration to persons with good posture verses not with those who have poor posture. Posture also affects our health since "hunching" crunches the abdomen and shoulders limiting the flow of the blood, lymph and endocrine delivery. Additionally, the throat chakra, the Vishudha, corresponds to our ability to project and receive energy. If we are "hunched" the throat center may be closed or constricted and we have a difficult time expressing ourselves and being heard. Personally, I do private readings seated and gallery sessions standing. I find standing not only allows me to remain aware of my posture but to keep moving around the room and, thereby, keep the energy moving. Since I make it a habit to be aware of my posture I find that when I begin to "hunch" a little red flag goes off in my head telling me to become aware of how the spirit is affecting me and question whether they are making inroads into me attempting to "take over." This brings me to another collateral issue for us to be attentive to.

When as a new reader, through developing familiarity in performing our skill, we begin to receive encouraging responses from our client; we tend to trust more in the direction that the spirit may take rather than following our individually developed reading protocol. In other words, in receiving positive reinforcement from our client we may tend to lean toward the relinquishing of directional control of the reading to the spirit. One of my contemporaries used to call this becoming a "victim of spirit." Spirits are people just like us except that they don't have a physical body to contend with. This being said, this should make it apparent to us all that any tendency toward manipulating others that they may have had in physical life will, more than likely, continue in their spirit life. Just because someone has crossed over does not indicate that they have matured any more than when they were here. In this respect, the same vigilance that we maintain with our clients we must also maintain with the spirits that we communicate with. We must not allow the spirit to "run" the reading. Additionally, this will allow us to be watchful for indications that we might be slipping into trance.

In staying attentive toward our posture, temperature, physical sensations, including taste and smell, and generally, any perceptions that can be considered "not us" we maintain our centeredness and a strong clear channel free of possible annexing influences. Essentially, we are an antenna. We must stay tuned to our channel and free of any "outside" distractions while "listening", in a detached manner, for pertinent information from our communicating spirit.

Staying in channel can pretty well assure us that we will know the difference between our client and the spirit in what we receive. We will know because the client usually projects more emotion than would a spirit sensed through channel. Hence, we will have a clear recognition of where information is coming from. If we begin to recognize that we are feeling what our client is feeling we should be attentive to the possibility that we might be starting to slip out of channel as this is a warning that empathy is gaining a better foothold.

As we become more familiar in working with our individually developed reading protocol we will use less energy being attentive to the details of discipline and have more energy available to "listen" more deeply. Discriminating which mode the spirit is communicating with us through (auditory, visual, olfactory, taste and tactile) becomes much easier to accomplish. Recognizing the need to switch modes is even more difficult for the accomplished reader, let alone, the beginner. Don't be discouraged if you don't catch on quickly. This takes a long time to develop. The more you "see your body as who you are" the more difficult this will be. Hence, the more you meditate or work in an artistic format, the easier it will come. Paying attention to which mode the information is being received through will, also, assist in the overall connection to the spirit and, consequently, strengthen the channel.

Lastly, a reminder; rely most on your client's interpretation of meaning since it will be more appropriate to their or the spirit's experience. If your client can't arrive at an interpretation offer yours but DON'T PUSH!

Part Five

HEALING BETWEEN the PLANES

A FEW WORDS ABOUT HEALING

In these days and times and in the current perspectives utilized throughout the metaphysical fields healing has evolved into being viewed from many different perspectives. The sheer numbers of such only serve to confirm the confusion in coming to a common understanding of what it is or is not. Everyone seems to have their own idea. I'm no different. In offering my own opinion here I am in no way asserting that anyone else's perspective is either right or wrong. I am simply offering an opinion which I will build upon throughout the rest of this section. If you are of a different opinion, please keep an open mind and at least hear what I have to offer. Broadening our perspectives is an ongoing process and must remain personally selective according to how you wish to structure your skills.

The state in which a person, spirit, place or thing exists with the most integrated and harmonious flow of energy can be considered to be a state of "good" health. If misaligned, the act of returning that person, spirit, place or thing to that state can be considered healing. This seems like a straight forward definition of what healing is until we consider what our baseline for assessment is. To date there seems to be no scientific or metaphysical agreement available to set any standards other than the hardcore physical data from the medical field which mostly lacks the inclusion of energy, or chi, emotional, mental and

93

psychological influences. This still leaves the current definition, for our purposes, within the realm of the theoretical. Theoretically and philosophically, healing or health now falls into the realm of perception. In light of the fact that it is said that beauty is in the eye of the beholder, might we also assume, then, that health is in the feeling of the perceiver? In the final analysis, if we don't feel "good" how can we believe that we are healthy? We must, then, assume that in returning a person, spirit, place or thing back to a state where it feels good to the perceiver must, in some way, be healing. Hence, someone healing from a wound, recovering from a loss, assimilating the effects of a perceived punishment, self-imposed or not, can all be said to be in process of healing. To take this a step further, not only is your client, most likely, healing from a loss but the spirit on the other side of the veil may be healing or in need of healing as well. How, you might ask, can a spirit need healing? First, the spirit is recovering from the loss of the "living" and physical life. Additionally, if they have regrets about how they left this plane they may be punishing themselves for acting or not acting in ways they believed they should have before leaving. In a sense you might say they have put themselves into a kind of purgatory. Purgatory is a derivative of the verb to purge, and what is being purged is whatever it is that is blocking the condition of feeling healthy. That could be guilt, regret or any other feeling associated with an unsatisfying, untimely or unexpected departure. In the metaphysical field, the most common terminology for this purging is called clearing. A general understanding of clearing was covered in Part 2. Please review this section before we proceed.

You as the reader can assist, in three ways by clearing environments, persons and "attached" spirits.

CLEARING ENVIRONMENTS

In reviewing the section on clearing you will remember that a piece of furniture can hold a feeling of depression, joy or a whole host of feelings deposited by the previous occupant(s). In the same way, any intense emotional projection, such as shock, anger, fear, may also be deposited, not only on a piece of furniture, but in a space within an environment. Think of a traffic intersection. A traffic accident would certainly qualify as having emotionally charged content that could be deposited in a space. To start with, we have the accident participants. The emotions generated would certainly be enough to be perceived but add physical injuries and the intensity and hype contributed by EMS and the local authorities and you now have a mix of emotions that are, literally, compounded on an exponential scale. Remember that with energy the whole is greater than the sum of the parts. Even rubberneckers contribute to the mix. And, odds are, once a space has been permeated with this vibration the Law of Attraction comes into play and more accidents will take place in the same space through the attraction. The energy deposit will snowball. In addition to injury, traumatic passings in any environment can produce a perceivable effect, not only on the environment but, on those who are sensitive and produce an unconscious reactive effect in those who are not.

To clear a space of any vibration, but not the memory or imprint, is much the same as spring cleaning. Energy aware people will call it clearing. Regardless of what we call it, it should be done every quarter year when the Sun passes the cardinal points in the zodiac (equinoxes and solstices). This way the "trapped" energy is released and available for new endeavors. Otherwise it is locked up as tension in the environment and often blocks the effectiveness of new projects by absorbing the newly applied energy through attraction. Under passive conditions any accumulation of energy will gradually dissipate of its own accord while not being "renewed" through repetitive action and with the arrival of other vibrations that overshadow it. Within one year's cycle most areas will clear themselves through neglect and without our input. It should be noted that, as we are all creatures of habit, at the same time each year we tend to repeat behaviors we generated in prior years. If you doubt this, examine your history for the past ten or fifteen years asking yourself what times of the year you made specific kinds of changes like beginnings and endings of relationships, jobs, illnesses, etc. This would be a very profitable project to undertake, from a personal perspective, as it will give you tremendous insight into your own common patterns of approach to differing circumstances based on what you are feeling at different times of the year. Let's move back to the issue of clearing.

If the intensity of the energy deposited is emotionally charged and is enough to linger long enough to allow more of its own type to be attracted, as within the space of a traffic accident or traumatic passing, intervention will be required. This is where we come in. This type of clearing can be performed on site or through absentee healing methods. On site is the most effective and participating as a group even more so. Since energy follows thought, this is a relatively easy exercise to do. In order to perform the exercise in the way I will describe it will be necessary to understand a few facts about energy.

Energy and light are the same thing. One of the reasons we consider them different is that we are only familiar with light in the visible spectrum. This is due to the range of what our eyes are physically able to perceive. The visible spectrum, however, is a very narrow spread of frequencies and the range of light and frequencies goes much further than what we are able to see. Scientists have said that all light/energy travels in waves. But if we look at those waves in all three dimensions, not just on a flat piece of paper, we find that the movement is, actually, more like a corkscrew. When we use a corkscrew to open a bottle of wine we find that when we turn the corkscrew clockwise, it goes down into the cork or away from us. When we turn the corkscrew counter clockwise, it turns up and away from the cork or towards us. So, from your point of visual reference, energy turning clockwise moves away from you and energy turning counter clockwise moves toward you. With this in mind, let's move on to our exercise.

With any area to be cleared its best that you have had visual and/or physical contact with it. If you haven't, go there to get a sense of the area. In this way you can recall the image and the feeling of the area within yourself later if you are unable perform the exercise on site. Without previous contact, any information you can acquire detailing the area will be helpful. Some readers merely need an address to "zero in" on the location, some need much more. Any exercises learning to utilize remote viewing would be highly useful for this or any absentee healing. The more tangible validation you have, the better directed will be the energies of your exercise. Before we go further, review the use of the workplace and the energy screen in the tools section of this manual.

First, move into your workspace. Whatever settling, grounding or mediation you need to get centered, do it in your workplace so as to feel relaxed and to insulate yourself from extraneous environmental influences. Put yourself into channel. When you are centered and comfortable, move to the table holding your energy screen, turn it on, tune it up and bring a picture of the area onto the screen. Pull the white light energy, simultaneously, up through your feet and down through your crown merging at your heart and project it from your heart while bathing the area to be cleared. At the same time you do this you will see it happening on your energy screen. Do this until you feel that you have filled the area enough to where it is completely saturated. Your area now has enough clean energy for you to do your work. Next, adjust your energy screen so that you are looking down on the area to be cleared. Still pulling the energy in through your crown and your feet merge it at the throat and project blue light spiraling down through the area in a clockwise (away from you) direction and down into the ground. Since the throat is the center of the will, this will serve to ground anything that is erratic or that runs contrary to the area's natural flow. Do this until you feel that there is no longer any resistance to what you are projecting. At this point you will feel the projection start to slow and dissipate. Now, soften your feel. Still pulling the energy in through the crown and the feet, again, merge it at the heart but this time softly emanate a pink light and spin it counterclockwise (toward you) that it may soften and gently permeate the area making it less dense, or as our colloquial metaphysical language calls it, "raising the energy." Since pink is the color of acceptance it will help release anything left that might tend to constrict the natural flow of energy in the area. As this energy softens and becomes transparent it begins to shift to the Creators color, gold. Bathe it in this energy until it feels comfortable to you. The area should now be cleared, grounded and naturally charged. If you're finished, shut off your energy screen and move away from your workplace unless you've other work to do.

Occasionally, you may have to repeat this process to remove those "stubborn stains." With practice this will become as second nature to you. The easiest and most dramatic results can be obtained by visualizing this in a unified projecting group of practitioners.

Essentially, we are washing away what we can, neutralizing what can't be washed away and lightening the vibration on what's left. It's important to note that even after doing the exercise a number of times and it has been returned to a natural flow of its own energy, the "memory" or residue of the conflicting energy will remain. It has essentially been imprinted with the prior experience as we might. We know the memory of our experiences will never leave but their effects can be diminished to a minimum.

Another fundamental concept in understanding the dynamics of energy is that energy follows thought. It is essential to understand that since energy = attention, wherever we put our attention, our energy will also go. Hence, anything we focus on receives enough energy to incite action relative to the current of thought(s). In Part I spoke about the Law of Attraction concerning the need for protection. Essentially, whatever we project, we will attract. So, if we project health, love and compassion we will attract the same. If we project fear, anger and worry, we will also attract more of the same. In the same way, then, when we focus on a location that needs to be cleared, we are drawing the energy of that place to us, and us to it, through the Law of Attraction. The focus, or thought, allows us to create an energy "link" or conduit to that location allowing us to work with the energy contained there. Thinking of or visualizing the location creates a specific intensity of attraction. If we were to also verbalize the name of the location out loud we add another dimension of focus; auditory or sound vibration. This dramatically increases the intensity of the "link" we have created to the location. This is very much like focusing the lens on a microscope or telescope. This allows a stronger and clearer connection promoting a much stronger response to whatever we are projecting. So, when we clear a space or a person, verbalizing the name of the person or space creates much more effective work. Additionally, if we have a possession of the person or an object or substance from the space, this would further increase the effectiveness or our work through an additional dimension of connection; tactile. Each dimension of added connection adds to the intensity of the connection and, hence, the effectiveness of our work and, correspondingly, the necessity for our own grounding of equal intensity when our work has been concluded.

CLEARING PEOPLE

Clearing people is not as straight forward as clearing a space. In clearing a space, it is either successful or not. With people, we are also dealing with their unconscious and may receive a variety of reactions from those undergoing the clearing.

Generally, people want to be cleared of whatever they feel blocks them from "feeling better" than they have. Often times, however, what they need to let go of is not something that they feel totally secure in doing. As a case in point, if a client loses a parent, the adult part of the client knows, and is agreeable to, the fact that the proper and "mature" thing to do, especially as non-verbally required by our social milieu, is to let go of any dependencies shared with the departed parent. However, the child within the adult, who is going to be much more emotional and less likely to be rational, will have a great deal of difficulty doing so. Publicly there is total agreement but privately, and most likely subconsciously, there may exist complete resistance. This resistance is felt as fear or anger and shows itself through justification, sarcasm, crying, laughing and outbursts of varying degree intended to stop the change while cloaked below the threshold of awareness so as not to risk confrontation. The client wishes to avoid open confrontation since that would lead to the embarrassment of admitting that they're not willing to do what is socially expected. Some clients are able to deal with these issues openly. Others, like this example, are not. Since child/parent rapport is different with every family, the range and intensity of possible responses is tremendous. I offer this explanation not as an opportunity to remedy the situation but as an understanding that in clearing people we must always be prepared for and we must always expect the unexpected. Having addressed this potential for reactions, let's move on to what we will be assisting people to clear themselves of. I say assist because with people must let go of what we are clearing. We simply alter the environment so they can feel what it is like to be cleared. It is up to them to sustain the feeling and the process.

Essentially, whatever it is that blocks a person from growing into their personal path is something that they can be aided with in clearing. First, however, there must be an honest desire, on their part, to get past the blockage. One of the first prerequisites of all healing (of which clearing is a part) is that we must have our client's acknowledgement to proceed. Whatever we can aid those in clearing will be something that is the result of their own creating. That is, it will have been internally generated by them, and most likely, in reaction to a loss. This is one of the reasons why it's important that they acknowledge the clearing. A statement of intention makes it clear to their unconscious what is offered by us.

The natural reaction of a human to any painful event is to clench, whether it is physical, emotional or intellectual. Hence, any pain is met with an attempt to contain it, effectively, immobilizing or "petrifying" the energy so the pain cannot progress any further.

Depression is, literally, the cessation of energy movement. Fear can create the same effect. When energy movement stops the intellect, emotions and body are, literally, starved of what they need to live and grow. This is why a person claiming to be depressed complains of having no energy to act. This is the first step toward the development of disease if allowed to continue. The application of energy by the reader helps to relax the clenching effect. The client's acknowledging of the clearing, consequently, reprograms their mind to aid the clearing by their unclenching. As the energy begins to flow again the client begins to clear their obstructions to living themselves.

What is being cleared has many names but will almost always show itself as some fashion of obstruction to the energy flow. We can call these conditions depression, fear, phobias, addictions, shyness, anger, prejudice, procrastination and ad infinitum. The bottom line, however, is that they all, to some extent, inhibit the energy flow. They exist on both conscious and unconscious levels and whether they are acknowledged by the client or not they are equally effective at obstruction. One of the major concepts to be understood, by the facilitator, is that the client is always, at least partially if not totally, liable for the obstruction, that is, they allow the condition to occur and/or persist through their choice of options. One exception might be young children as they have not yet developed the ability and experience to choose except as through a reactive animal nature. Accountability, confrontation and fear of success are at the core of their choices. The more externally oriented the motivations of a client are, the more likely it is that they will avoid being accountable by denying that they ever had another option. For them, to react obstructively retains, for them, a measure of security and comfort in the familiarity of the circumstance even though the situation itself may produce pain. The pain of what is known is preferable to the possibility of unknown pain fueled by their imaginary "what ifs" concerning being accountable and confronting. Conversely, the client that is motivated through their own internal assessment of being responsible for their situation is much more likely to respond constructively to clearing, and actually aid in doing so, since they have acknowledged that there is an issue to be dealt with and that they are willing to confront it. Part of our challenge is knowing when to act as a psychologist in attempting to make the unaware and the unaccountable client aware that they have the keys to clear their situation and that they are fully capable of assimilating and handling the conditions that go along with the new energy. It is very difficult for us, especially for the unaccountable client, to develop Self-Trust when we give deference to the external world for determining what we will accept as valued. Aside from this perspective, the best a facilitator can hope to achieve through offering clearing to any person is to provide, temporarily, a safe space for them to feel what it's like to be clear without being influenced by the assumed expectations of others.

Whether our client is aware or not and acknowledging or not, the process for clearing will remain the same except in that the one who acknowledges the need will not block us through their denial. Let's move on to the exercise.

To clear a client it's best to have visual and/or proximity contact with them. If not, absentee healing, conducted through remote viewing, will be almost as effective. Without contact, any information you can acquire detailing the person and their issues will be helpful. A name vibration is, usually, sufficient to make a cogent connection.

First, move into your workspace. Whatever settling, grounding or mediation you need to get centered, do it in your workplace so as to feel relaxed and to insulate yourself from extraneous environmental influences. Put yourself into channel. When you are centered and comfortable, move to the table holding your energy screen, turn it on, tune it up and bring a picture of your client on to the screen. Once the client's image is on the screen, before you do anything else, ask the image if they will accept the clearing that you intend to perform and watch for their reaction. If you receive an affirmative reaction, nod of the head, thumbs up, etc., continue on. If not, DO NOT proceed. On your energy screen, pull white light, simultaneously, up through their feet and down through their crown merging at their heart. Using your breath, expand it out from their heart bathing their entire body and a short distance beyond encompassing their aura. Do this until you feel that their space is completely saturated. There is, now, enough clean energy available to fuel the clearing. Still pulling the energy down through their crown, change the tinting to a midnight blue and spiral it down around them in a clockwise direction. From your perspective this will appear to move down and left to right behind them and right to left in front of them. Do this until you feel that there is no longer any resistance to the induced flow. Shortly, you will feel the motion start to slow and dissipate. Now, soften your feel. Feel a shift from blue to pink and reverse the flow while spiraling the energy up through their feet toward their crown in a counterclockwise direction. From your perspective this will appear to move up and left to right in front of them and right to left behind them. When the pink becomes more translucent, you'll know that it has softened and gently permeated their aura making it less dense. Again, as our colloquial metaphysical language calls it, we have aided in "raising their energy." Since pink is the color of acceptance it will help release any residue that might tend to constrict their natural flow of energy. As this energy continues to soften and become transparent it begins to shift to gold still moving up and counterclockwise. Continue to bathe them in this energy until they appear relaxed and comfortable. They are now as cleared, grounded and naturally charged as you will be able to assist with. It is now up to them to retain what it feels like to be clear of the targeted issues and should now be able to repeat the clearing from memory by recreating the feeling. When you're finished, shut off your energy screen and move away from your workspace.

SPIRIT or ENTITY ATTACHMENT?

Any imbalance or disease is the result of a process. It has taken time for us to build an imbalanced pattern that will physically manifest itself. When we drop seeds for a crop in a field with no preparation, there certainly is a possibility for that crop to grow and prosper but how much better are the chances if we til and fertilize the soil and water the seed? To tend a garden means, literally, to give it "at-tend-tion." Why should any imbalance or disease be any different? The idea that we "catch a cold" implies that whatever ails us is a result of something that has externally assaulted us and taken hold through no fault of our own. We, then, allow ourselves to assume that we are somehow free of blame or are innocent of its cause and thereby deserving of some relief of our malady. Nothing could be further from the truth. The fact that we become imbalanced or ill in any way is testimony to the fact that we have tilled and fertilized the soil and watered the seed of whatever grows in our garden. Generally, illness cannot survive in the environment of a healthy immune system. If we become ill or imbalanced we must, truthfully, ask ourselves, "What have we done, or not, to contribute to its growth and prosperity?" If we look back we can, undoubtedly, see where we did not administering fertilizer, water and rest to our immune system by eating junk food, not getting enough sleep and pushing ourselves past the breaking point with the addition of mental, emotional and physical stress.

At this point you're probably asking yourself what has this to do with spirit attachment, right? Before I answer that, I want you to ask yourself a question. What kinds of people do self-destructive people attract to them? There are two. "Do-gooders" and those who wish to accelerate the destruction. Why? It's because both of them wish to feed off the resources that are being released as a result of the destruction. Let's go back to our definition of "good" health. It's the state in which a person, spirit, place or thing exists with the most integrated and harmonious flow of energy. When we diminish ourselves, in any way, we are no longer integrated nor have we a harmonious flow of energy. In doing so we are, essentially, wasting the energy and resources that we need to keep ourselves healthy and integrated. When this occurs, it's like a broadcast on the "airwaves" to the "bottom feeders" that there is free "manna" for those looking for an energy feast. "Bottom feeders" can be people who are in the physical or deceased. This is the same rule that applies to nature. When an animal is injured or dying, they attract predators that sense that they are in a weakened state and easy prey. Yet, predators are not evil. When a cat eats a mouse, are they evil? Of course not! They're just following their natural survival instincts. Animal life is survival of the fittest. We are also part animal. When we waste our resources in activities and diminish ourselves we are, essentially, putting ourselves in a "wounded" state that attracts predators.

One last concept before we move on to define our spirit attachment. This diminishing or self-destructive behavior is, usually, not conscious. That is, we are, often, not aware that we are diminishing ourselves. We may simply know that we don't feel well, but not know why or how to change it. How might this manifest? It might show itself as neglecting our diet, maintaining addictions to things that sap our vitality, contributing to gossip, refusing to let go of situations and behaviors that are counter constructive and disempowering, holding on to fear, depression and anger and any other choice of behavior that runs contrary to feeling healthy and compromises our healthy flow of energy.

Now, what is spirit attachment? It is any symbiotic connection between entities that contributes to blocking or siphoning off the natural movement of a healthy and naturally evolving energy.

Let's look at an example. If a client has lost someone important to them, their self-image or direction is in flux and they may be unable or unwilling to let the spirit leave. Their need for the deceased is still strong since they haven't processed their passing. The client and the deceased spirit are then said to be in mourning and grieving. This is natural. There is nothing wrong with a residue attachment and their feeling that way and, over time, they will grieve and, eventually, let each other move on. However, if over a long period of time the client and/or the spirit has been unable or unwilling to process the loss through grieving the attachment may become their normal way of being. This attachment, which was natural, now becomes pathological. Relating in a retentive and symbiotic way becomes a crutch for a "protected" existence and an excuse not to evolve past the relationship. Do you remember the lady I spoke about who went from medium to medium attempting to reconnect with her dead son? This is an attachment in a pathological form. For some reason she is unable to let go. Her son may have grieved and evolved, we don't know for sure, but she, apparently, has not. This is emotional illness. Remember the garden? Her tilling, fertilizing, watering and tending has grown this attachment past her ability to break free on her own. She now can't help herself. From her perspective, she needs the attachment to survive. There are probably many possible reasons why she fostered the attachment, but from my perception, I have personally deduced two possibilities. There may be some form of guilt over his passing and/or she may be unwilling to look at the life issues remaining and dealing with her current husband or younger child. Realize also that her son is unable to move on and evolve due to the mother's unwillingness to let him go. In either case, the natural evolution of these two situations has been blocked. If allowed to continue, these emotional blockages will, inevitably, contribute to her having a physical manifestation of illness. The illness will occur in whatever bodily system is the weakest and/or has the strongest hereditary predisposition for failure. She has been recommended to professional help but has refused to partake. Her future health is in her hands.

There are other forms of attachment. With the addict who has a physical dependency there is also a mental and emotional counterpart which has paved the way for attachment. Who might be attached to the addict you might ask? That would be any spirit that was previously addicted before they departed and would need to feel the "high" accomplished through the physical body previously used. These spirits would, most likely, be trapped on the emotional plane through their desire and past actions and, therefore, still subject to their need, but now, only from a mental and emotional perspective. Remember, next to the etheric, the emotional plane is the closest to the physical. The physical vehicle could be drugs, alcohol, food, sex or any substance or behavior that could provide some form of "rush" and, temporarily, fulfill the left over emotional desire. This spirit would encourage the client into behavior that would stimulate the circumstances that contribute toward the addiction. The client may feel urges, not necessarily his own, that would lead him to do things leading to the addictive satisfaction. If the client is not in the habit of checking his temperature as described previously, and most people don't, they will feel the "fed" urges as their own and simply react to them. The result will be that they can, symbiotically, enable each other's codependent behavior. Again, this is a pathological attachment. Both, the client and the spirit, need help in breaking the destructive cycle.

Both of these examples are circumstances that contribute to issues of dependency and codependency. Both can be viewed as pathological since neither the spirits nor the clients appear to be either willing or able to break free of the dependency without some form of assistance from outside the attachment. Remember, the spirit is only minus a body. They still have the capacity of forming emotional habits which can be difficult to break.

There are other connections between spirit and client which are not to be regarded as pathological or attachments. Our connection to our guide, for example, is not one of dependency but, perhaps, one of tutelage. Both we and the guide seek each other out by choice, not as a response to a need. However, we may occasionally assist each other in times of need. We may have friends and relatives in spirit that we occasionally "converse" with in love and support. Granted, any relationship, even beyond those of us who have passed into spirit, have the potential to develop into dependencies, but, this is usually, not the case. It only becomes pathological, or an attachment, when we become unable to function normally or become immobilized without the input of the other. As long as you use common sense, you should have little trouble distinguishing between the two.

The exercise for detaching spirit attachments is essentially the same as that of clearing clients, but that you will, additionally, need to apply energy to the attachment. This action will take much more energy and much more perseverance than a typical client clearing since you can be fuel for the two of them. The principle concept is to feed the attachment enough clean energy that they "let go" of the client for a time. In the interim of this detachment it is necessary to "beef up" your client's psychic immune system, as much as you can, by helping them to build better self-confidence and recognize their situation before the attachment is no longer sated by what you have previously fed them and returns to your client for a refill. Since your client's pattern has built up slowly over a long period of time it may take many sessions to enable them to build their defenses by assisting in the increase their self-confidence. They may, also, require the assistance of others who have your client's wellbeing at heart.

There is one major precaution that must be recognized if you are to undertake spirit detachment. In extreme cases, this is very much like an exorcism. The amount of energy, stamina and strength of character required for this is much more than the capacity of the typical medium. It is not for everyone to perform. It takes a unique strength of character to not become the target of transference for the client's parasite. That is, if you are inexperienced or weak in your character and channel strength, you many become the target of the attachment. Remember, through your training, you have learned to provide clean "higher octane" energy than the average person. Feeling supercharged is not, necessarily, an indication that you possess the tenacity required. Think long and hard about your motives and abilities before you decide to get involved. There is no shame in referring a case of attachment or possession to someone who is better experienced and more qualified. Don't be a hero or you may end up needing one.

SOUL or SPIRIT RETRIEVAL

Soul or spirit retrieval is a bit different in that it is a very simple process. When we pass, our mental and emotional state usually doesn't change much between the time we leave and the time we recognize that we have "arrived" somewhere else. Whatever emotional state we are in when we discorporate will probably be the same state we begin with in our "new place." If we feel that we've led a "good" life and passing was easy we may find being on the other side of the veil very comforting and perhaps a bit of an adventure. If, on the other hand, we left feeling regretful, we will probably arrive feeling, somehow, undeserving of or not entitled to enjoy the new experience. All of us know the feeling of when we have felt badly about how we have handled a situation that seems to perpetuate itself as a stubborn reminder in our consciousness, like a closed loop video, replaying over and over and creating a very frustrating and self-criticizing view of our experience. Because of our judgment, whether self-generated or accepted from others, we find ourselves trapped in, what I call, a mind lock. That is, we are unable to focus on anything else, let alone, how to allow ourselves to perceive the situation in a different framework that will allow us to evolve and move past it. This becomes a kind of self-imposed purgatory. We also know that, when we connect with another person who is neither aware of what our focus is nor wants to "go there" if they are aware, we are, intentionally or unintentionally, pulled, by them, into another focus, thereby, breaking the loop. Essentially, we become distracted from focusing on our self-indicting judgments. Whether we are incarnate or not, everyone seems to be susceptible to this kind of dilemma. The solution seems to be nothing short of simply refocusing the energy we apply onto something more enjoyable or constructive. For the incarnate, this can be accomplished through some form of therapist or aware friend. For the discarnate, this can be accomplished through a loved one's prayers or the questions of a medium. Prayer is, simply, directing love and energy to someone who is felt to be in need of it. The prayer provides enough energy and encouragement for the spirit to choose to overcome their current limitation. Prayer is very much like someone getting a "pep-talk" from a caring and compassionate friend. The only drawback is that it is up to the one receiving the "pep-talk" or prayer to use the energy to make the choice to refocus. The medium goes one step further than just applying an availability of energy to fuel their potential choice to break free. He or she can perform a kind of mental or emotional sleight of hand by asking the spirit questions that will, distract them from the loop and encourage them to focus on other aspects and accomplishments that they can feel good about from their previous life. This trick breaks the mind lock or loop without any coercion or force. When this occurs they can, usually, evolve past their own limiting and hurtful self-judgments. This requires a minimum amount of energy. This may also need to be done a few times, especially, if the circumstance dwelled upon has intensity.

As an example, I will cite my first experience of becoming aware of performing soul or spirit retrieval. In the history of a very close friend, a grandmother had passed years earlier. When my friend encountered her on the astral plane she looked worn, depressed and had, what appeared to be, black circles around her eyes. Needless to say, she appeared to need all the prayer and energy she could acquire. Upon connecting with her through spirit communication we learned that she was extremely regretful about how she had handled the upbringing of my friend's father. She couldn't apologize enough and wanted my friend to carry that message back to him. My friend acknowledged the request and we continued on with the session. Mind you, my objective was not focused on a healing but on making the connection, refining my skill and acquiring some information for my friend. As we moved on the focus changed to her earlier life and her love for cooking. We received impressions of iron pots, family dinners, seating arrangements, types of food cooked and conversations and circumstances surrounding the meal events. Upon closing the session we found the grandmother with substantially less eye darkening, better posture, quicker and more agile movements and a departure where she actually left smiling. My friend and I were very excited and discussed at length what had occurred. It was then that we discovered this method of healing, yet, we had no name for it until we encountered another medium whose repertoire it was part of.

It should be mentioned that soul or spirit retrieval will, most likely, be necessary with or after removing spirit attachments. Because of how the retrieval works, it can be considered a confidence and self-concept booster which is necessary for loosening the grip of a client's attachments. Once you are aware as to whether the client has put themselves into purgatory or had some help from a discouraging spirit, or both, carefully think through how you and your client would like to proceed in order to eliminate the degenerative influences and to strengthen their self-concept and their psychic immune system to prevent further "infestation." Essentially, there is little difference between this and setting up medication and a quarantine to prevent the spread of a disease. Let common sense and your intuition be your guide.

IN SUMMARY

This book is the coagulation of many personal discoveries, life experiences, soul searching and acquired understandings. The friends, clients and associations I have come in contact with have all been my teachers and in no way, can I lay claim to any of this knowledge as being my own. These understandings, and much more, should be common knowledge to those of us who are aspiring to be more than what our animal nature has endowed us with.

APPENDIX I

PROGRESSIVE RELAXATION

Find a quiet place where you can relax and remain uninterrupted. If this is leading into a meditation or going into channel, it's best if you sit up with your back straight. If you prefer to lie down, do so in a place other than your bed unless you are using the exercise to prepare for sleep. If you attempt to meditate or go into channel in your bed, you will have a difficult time doing so. Why? What do you do in your bed? What is the residue vibration left there? Need I say more? I would suggest that you record your own CD of the following dialogue. We are much more comfortable letting go with our own voice than that of others. You may also get someone else to record whose voice you find comforting and relaxing. In lieu of these options, you may also purchase a CD from the Astrological Institute. The dialogue, here, follows a progression similar to the one on the Monroe CDs. Let's move on to the dialogue.

"Sit comfortably with your back straight and feet flat on the floor. Feel the weight of your body in the chair.

"Inhale through the nose while expanding your belly.

"As you exhale, let the weight of your body be what gently pushes the air out.

"Again, inhale through the nose while expanding your belly.

"As you exhale, let the weight of your body be what gently pushes the air out.

"Once more, inhale through the nose while expanding your belly.

"As you exhale, let the weight of your body be what gently pushes the air out.

"Breathe normally. Feel your body "melting" into the chair.

"In your mind's eye, step outside of yourself and look at yourself.

"As you do, you see a point of white light appear in the center of your heart.

"As you breathe, you see this point of white light pulsate to the rhythm of your breath.

"As you inhale, you see this light expand to encompass your heart, your chest, your shoulders, your abdomen, back and hips, your cheeks, legs and feet. Expanding further you include your arms, wrists, hands and fingers, your neck and your head until you are completely encompassed by clean, clear, healing white light.

"Relax now for a few moments and enjoy the cool, calm feeling of relaxation all though your body.

"As you open your inner eyes, you see before you your Worry Box. Place in the box all your worries, cares and concerns. You won't need them now and they'll simply get in the way. Do this now while I wait.

"Now, close the lid on your Worry Box and push it around behind you out of sight.

"Let's begin, now, our ten point exercise for relaxation.

"One, your mind tells your jaw, all the muscles, nerves and vessels, in your jaw to relax. "Let go, go limp and sleep. And…your jaw obeys.

"Your mind tells your cheeks, each cheek, to relax, let go, go limp and sleep.

"Your mind tells your forehead, all the furls and burrows in your forehead to relax, let go, go limp and sleep.

"Your mind tells your eyes, all the muscles nerves and vessels in your eyes, relax, let go and go limp.

"Two, your mind tells the back of your neck, all the muscles, nerves and vessels in the back of your neck to relax, let go, go limp and sleep.

"Your mind tells your scalp and ears, all the muscles, nerves and vessels in your scalp and ears to relax, let go, go limp and sleep.

"Three, now let this relaxation, let this relaxation throughout your head, neck and face, let this relaxation penetrate inward, inward, inward so your brain feels deeply relaxed and your mind is bright, awake and alert.

"Four, as you open your mind's eye and look down at your feet, your mind tells your feet, all the muscles, nerves and vessels in your feet, relax, let go, go limp and sleep.

"Five, your mind tells your legs, your calves, shins and thighs, your mind tells your legs relax, let go, go limp and sleep.

"Six, your minds tells your lower body, your hips, your genitals, your cheeks, your intestines and bladder, your minds tells your lower body, relax, let go, go limp and sleep.

"Seven, your mind tells all the organs in your middle body, your stomach, your kidneys, your liver, your spleen, your mind tells the organs in your middle body, relax, let go, go limp and sleep.

"Eight, your mind tells all the organs in your upper body, your heart, your chest, your lungs, and your mind tells all the organs in your upper body, relax, let go, go limp and sleep.

"Nine, your mind tell your shoulders, your upper back, your upper arms, forearms, wrists, hands and fingers, your mind tells all these parts, relax, let go, go limp and sleep.

"Ten, ten, ten, you are now in a state of deep relaxation, where your body is deeply and comfortably asleep and your mind is bright, awake and alert."

At this juncture you may insert any meditative or guided work that you wish. This progressive relaxation has enable a relaxed, cleared and grounded state that lends itself well to any work that requires the non-interference of the physical, emotional and mental planes of action. When you have concluded the intended work, add the dialogue, listed below, to smoothly return to waking consciousness which includes the physical, emotional and mental planes of action.

"Now, let's begin our ten count back to waking consciousness in this room.

"Ten. Inhale more deeply, that is, taking more air.

"Nine. Wiggle your fingers and your toes.

"Eight. Roll your head and neck on your shoulders, first one way, and then the other way.

"Seven. Inhale more deeply, that is, take in more air.

"Six. Roll your shoulders, first one way, and then the other way.

"Five. Inhale more deeply, that is, take in more air.

"Four. Twist your body on your seat so you feel the weight of your body in the chair.

"Three. Two. One. Wake up. Open your eyes. You are back in the room."

APPENDIX II

MEDITATION TO HIGHER SELF

"As you open your inner eyes, you see your workplace before you.

"Move to the entrance of your workplace, open the entrance, step through and close the entrance behind you.

"Move to the center of your workplace and take notice; what has changed since the last time you've been in your workplace?

"Now that you're in the center of your workplace, slowly inhale and as you do pull your inhale into your heart and see this white light grow in size, intensity and focus.

"And as you slowly exhale feel this light emanating, around you, outward, outward and outward until this exhaled white light is completely filling your workplace with your white light energy, your comfort zone, your protection zone, your recharge zone.

"Now, inhale again pulling that energy back into the heart and as you exhale, push this white light upward, through your body, out the crown of your head and spiral it up as far and as high as you can see and reach.

"And as you continue, to breathe this channel that comes from your heart center and out through the crown of your head and up as high as you can reach.

"It gets wider and wider until your body is completely surrounded by a cylinder of white light, surrounding and spinning around you, all the way down to your feet, up past your head and up, up, and up as high and as far as you can reach and feel.

"As you inhale and exhale again, feel yourself start to slowly spin from right to left, or counterclockwise.

"As this happens, you move up inside that cylinder.

"And as you go higher & higher, you recognize that you have arrived at a second level.

"Step out of the white light onto the platform of the second level room.

"It is surrounded by the same protection you have given your workplace.

"The channel coming up from below and continuing up is like and elevator.

"Let it continue in place.

"As your eyes become accustomed to being in the second level in the dimmer light, you look around.

"What you see are consoles with dials, switches and screens.

"You notice that one of these consoles is labeled Higher Self.

"Move toward that console.

"You notice a three position switch: off, standby and on.

"Move the switch into the on position.

"Next to the switch you see a dial that says volume.

"Turn this dial to a comfortable volume for you, knowing that at any time, if you are having difficulty hearing your Higher Self that you can immediately, with your breath, put yourself in this room and change the dial to whatever setting you need to cleanly, clearly and distinctly hear what your Higher Self is saying.

"Above that dial is another.

"It says Screen-Picture.

"Turn that dial on and to a comfortable visibility as your Higher Self comes onto the screen over that console.

"Set it to a comfortable brightness and size.

"Leave the screen, switches and dials in their current position and move back into the channel of white light.

"Again, feel yourself start to gently spin counterclockwise again and as you move up into the next level the light is getting brighter and brighter.

"It is almost blinding.

"Step out of the cylinder and onto the Guides' level which is saturated with white light.

"Step further into the space.

"Reach out with both hands asking your Protector and Life Guides to join you.

"Immediately, both hands are grasped by your Protector and your Life Guide.

"Look them both in the eyes and say, "Thank you for joining me."

"Let go of their hands, knowing that your guides are always with you when you ask for them.

"Move back into the cylinder of white light, step in and resume spinning.

"As you look down, feel your feet stretch down to the first floor of your workplace.

"As you look up, feel yourself stretch as high as you possibly can see.

"As you do, you see your Higher Self reaching down toward you.

"As you make the connection, a river of energy begins to flow, both up and down, through you like a tremendous electrical current.

"Leave a part of you in this place and slowly, let the other part of you descend, past the second or control level, down to the bottom floor or your workplace.

"Step outside the channel leaving everything intact and in place.

"Again, survey your workplace and take note if anything has changed.

"Move now to the entrance to your workplace.

"Open the entrance, step through and close the entrance behind you and start moving away from your workplace.

"Now, let's do our ten count back to waking consciousness in this room.

"When we come back to this room, all of your senses will be working cleanly, sharply and proficiently.

"You will remember everything that you have seen, heard, felt and done.

"And you will feel refreshed, energized, grounded and ready to do the day's work."

APPENDIX III

MEDITATION TO CONSTRUCT A CONTROL ROOM

"As you open your inner eyes, you see your workplace before you.

"Move to the entrance of your workplace, open the entrance, step through and close the entrance behind you.

"Move to the center of your workplace and take notice; what has changed since the last time you've been in your workplace?

"Now that you're in the center of your workplace, slowly inhale and as you do pull your inhale into your heart and see this white light grow in size, intensity and focus.

"And as you slowly exhale feel this light emanating, around you, outward, outward and outward until this exhaled white light is completely filling your workplace with your white light energy, your comfort zone, your protection zone, your recharge zone.

"Now as you inhale again pull that energy back into the heart and as you exhale, push this white light upward, through your body, out the crown of your head and spiral it up as far and as high as you can see and reach.

"And as you continue, breathe out this channel that comes from your heart center and out through the crown of your head and up as high as you can reach.

"It gets wider and wider until your body is completely surrounded by a cylinder of white light, surrounding and spinning around you, all the way down to your feet, up past your head and up, up, and up as high and as far as you can reach and feel.

"As you inhale and exhale again, feel yourself start to slowly spin from right to left, or counterclockwise.

"As this happens, you levitate up through that cylinder.

"The channel coming up from below and continuing up is like an elevator.

"As you go higher and higher, you recognize that you arrived at a second level.

"Step out of the white light onto the platform of the second level room.

"It is surrounded by the same protection you have given your workplace.

"Let it continue in place.

"As your eyes become accustomed to being in the second level in the dimmer light, you look around.

"What you see are consoles with dials, switches and screens.

"Move to the closest control station.

"As you read its label, it says audio.

"There is a three position switch on the console; off, standby and on.

"Make certain is in the on position.

"Turn the knob and raise the volume to a comfortable level.

"It's almost as if you can hear all the voices of the world, of your guides, of people who have passed and people who are living.

"There is another knob next to that one. As you turn that one up, it filters out the noise and helps you to receive only the voices from whom you wish to receive information from.

"You can adjust this knob so you can hear all the information, all the way down to hearing from only one person.

"Adjust it for your comfort and convenience.

"With your right hand, squeeze your right ear lobe.

"As you do, your world becomes silent as all sound ceases.

"Squeeze it again and everything resumes its previous level.

"This is your quick switch if you become overwhelmed.

"To your right there is another console to which you move.

"It's label says visual and there is a screen above it.

"As you adjust the first knob one way, the picture becomes brighter, and, as you turn it the other way, darker and more subdued.

"The next knob allows you to sharpen it to crystal clarity or soften it to a soft blur.

"And a third knob allows you to pan in and make the picture closer and pan out and make it seem farther away.

"With the fingers of your right hand touch your right eye.

"As you do, the whole picture goes dark.

"Touch it again and as you do, everything resumes the same brightness, clarity and closeness.

"This is your quick switch if you become overwhelmed.

"To your right there is third console to which you move.

"It's label says tactile and feeling.

"As you adjust the first knob you feelings and sensations become amplified and concentrated.

"As you adjust the knob in the other direction they become muted and subdued.

"Adjust it to a comfortable level.

"Touch the fingers of your right hand to the back of the left.

"As you do, the feelings simply disappear as if your body has become wrapped and insulated with cotton.

"Again, touch the back of your left with the fingers of your right.

"All the feelings and sensations return as they were.

"This is your quick switch if you become overwhelmed.

"To your right there is fourth console to which you move.

"Resting on it is a helmet wired to the console.

"Reach down and put the helmet on your head.

"As you slowly adjust the first knob that you find, you receive a flow of flashes composed of sight, sound and feeling.

"These are telepathic images.

"As you turn the knob further, they arrive at a faster and more intense pace.

"As you turn the knob the other way they arrive more slowly and almost at a one after the other pace.

"Touch the fingers of your right hand to your third eye.

"As you do, the image flow ceases.

"As you touch it again, the image flow resumes the same flow and intensity.

"This is your quick switch if you become overwhelmed.

"To your right there is fifth console, with a solitary button, to which you move.

"As you press this button, all sight, sound, sensory and telepathic input ceases.

"As you press it again, all sight, sound, sensory and telepathic input resumes its previous level.

"This is your panic switch if you become overwhelmed.

"Back away from the consoles and move toward the cylinder of white light.

"Step off the platform and into the cylinder.

"As you do, you gently begin to turn in a clockwise direction as you move down to the first level of your workplace.

"Again, survey your workplace and take note if anything has changed.

"Move now to the entrance to your workplace.

"Open the entrance, step through and close the entrance behind you and start moving away from your workplace.

"Now, let's do our ten-count back to waking consciousness in this room.

"When we come back to this room, all of your senses will be working cleanly, sharply and proficiently.

"You will remember everything that you have seen, heard, felt and done.

"And you will feel refreshed, energized, grounded and ready to do the day's work."

ACKNOWLEDGEMENTS

They say that the journey from the head to the heart is the longest one we will ever take. At this point in my life I can certainly agree with that, although I am still on the path between the two. Along this journey I have encountered many people; some of whom aggravated me, some left me cold and some were an inspiration and encouragement to me.

First, I would like to thank all of my students and clients who unwittingly consented to being the guinea pigs for my blundering through this field. I would like to thank Charles Filius who showed me that having a sense of humor is important on all the planes. I would like to express my gratitude to Ed Hicks and Jason Oliver who have shown me that the only way to expand the knowledge is to open the flower; willingly or not. I'd also like to thank John Edward, whose counsel and example has shown me that mediumship and spirit communication can be approached in a down to earth, practical and applicable fashion. I would also like to thank my former spouse and business partner, Sandy Anastasi, without whose combined daytime and late-night brainstorming, about how to present this material to our students in an honorable and safe way, this book would never have been possible.

Anastasi, Sandy. (2021). *Anastasi System of Psychic Development-Level 6. Healing Through Spirit Communication.* Sandy Anastasi, Inc., Pt. Charlotte, Fl. ISBN# 978-1-105727627.

Anderson, George & Barone, Andrew. (2000). *George Anderson's Lessons from the Light: Extraordinary Messages.* Berkley Publications Group. N.Y., N.Y. ISBN# 978-0-425174166.

Anderson, Susan. (2006). *Communication With Grace: The Awakening of a Psychic Medium.* Itasca Books, Minneapolis, Mn. ISBN# 978-0-976705451.

Brown, Sylvia. (1998). *Adventures of a Psychic: A Fascinating and True Life Story of One of America's Most Successful Clairvoyants.* Hay House, Carlsbad, Ca. ISBN# 978-1-561706211.

Edward, John, (2004). *After Life: Answers from the Other Side.* Princess Books, Littlestown, Pa. ISBN# 978-1-932128086.

Edward, John. (2002). *Crossing Over: The Stories Behind Stories.* Hay House, Carlsbad, Ca. ISBN# 978-1-932128000.

Edward, John. (1999). *One Last Time: A Medium Speaks.* Berkley Publications Group, N.Y., N.Y. ISBN# 978-0-425166925.

Edward, John. (2005). *Practical Praying: Using the Rosary to Enhance Your Life.* Hay House, Carlsbad, Ca. ISBN# 978-1-932128123.

Edward, John. (2004). *What if God Were the Sun?* Berkley Publications Group, N.Y., N.Y. ISBN# 978-1-932128017.

Filius, Charles A. (2007). *Selections from On a Wing and a Prayer*. Charles A. Filius, Ca. ISBN# 978-0-615177977.

Gonzalez-Wippler, Migene. (1951). *What Happens After Death? Scientific and Personal Evidence for Survival*. Llewellyn Publishers, Woodbury, Minn. ISBN# 978-1-567183276.

Guggenheim, Bill & Judy. (1997). *Hello From Heaven: A New Field of Research*. Bantam Books, N,Y., N.Y. ISBN# 978-0-553576344.

Kardec, Allan. (1970). *The Book on Mediums: A Guide for Mediums & Invocators*. Weiser Books, Cape Neddick, Me. ISBN# 978-0-877283829.

Martin, Joel & Romanowski, Patricia. (1994). *Our Children Forever: George Anderson's Messages from Children on the Other Side*. Berkley Trade, N.Y., N.Y. ISBN# 978-0-425141380.

Martin, Joel & Romanowski, Patricia. (1992). *We Are Not Forgotten: George Anderson's Messages of Love*. Berkley Publications Group, N.Y., N.Y. ISBN# 978-0-425132883.

Martin, Joel & Romanowski, Patricia. (2002). *We Don't Die: George Anderson's Conversations with the Other Side*. Berkley Publications Group, N.Y., N.Y. ISBN# 978-0-425184998.

Newton, PhD., Michael. (1994). *Journey of Souls: Case Studies of Life Between Lives*. Llewellyn Publications, Woodbury, Mn. ISBN# 978-1-5671-8484-3.

Newton, PhD., Michael. (2000). *Destiny of Souls: New Case Studies of Life Between Lives*. Llewellyn Publications, Woodbury, Mn. ISBN# 978-1-56718-499-0.

Northrop, Suzane & McLoughlin, Kate. (1995). *Séance: Healing Messages from Beyond*. Dell Books, Norwalk, Ct. ISBN# 978-0-440221760.

Roman, Sanaya. (1993). *How to Connect with Your Guide*. H.J.Kramer, Novato, Ca. ISBN# 978-0-915811052.

Schwartz, Gary. (2003). *After Life Experiments: Breakthrough Scientific Evidence of Life After Death*. Atria Books, N.Y., N.Y. ISBN# 978-0-743436595.

Van Praag, James. (1999). *Talking to Heaven: A Medium's Message of Life After Death*. Berkley Publications Group, N.Y., N.Y. ISBN# 978-0-451191724

ABOUT the AUTHOR

John Lawrence Maerz is an author, instructor and professional speaker with specializations in metaphysics and psychology. His extensive background in metaphysical disciplines includes astrology, tarot, numerology, I-Ching, energy work, martial arts, psychic development and mediumship.

John has worked as a counselor and case manager with teen substance abuse, in child protection services and is a seasoned personal coach and adviser with diverse experience in the field of human potential. He incorporates and integrates personality influences, shadow work, nutritional needs, creative expression and personal desires while uncovering his client's innate abilities and potential.

John co-owned and successfully ran Starchild, a metaphysical bookstore in Port Charlotte, Florida, from 1995-2005. He also co-owned and ran the Astrological Institute of Integrated Studies begun in Bayshore New York, a school teaching a multitude of metaphysical subjects from 1983-1989 and in Florida from 1989-2005. He is dedicated to raising awareness and sharing his own unique perspective and understanding about life's journey and its meaning. He recognizes and emphasizes the importance of having balance and accountability. He challenges his students and clients to keep fulfilling their spiritual potential through their own individual experiences.

Over the years, John has produced a series of books, workshops, lectures and seminars presenting different metaphysical topics in print and on MP3. These materials are available on JohnMaerz.com. He is also a voracious writer and has written more than 85 articles on many thought-provoking subjects which are also available on his site. He has also published fifteen books on metaphysics and psychology. All books are available through Amazon.

You can contact John at **(941) 286-1562**

or at **JM@JohnMaerz.com**

Made in the USA
Monee, IL
07 July 2026

56549085R00079